JOY
IN THE JOURNEY

SUSAN KOCAK

ISBN: 9798786479318

Printed in the United States of America

Published by Book Marketeers.com

Here I sit... my first book, meant to leave a legacy for my children and their children: *Adam, Jared, Joel, Dominick*, and *Annie*. Then along came *Kathryn, Joscelyn, Aly, Caroline*, and *Zak*. In time grandchildren entered...*Evianna, Jack, Alivia, Lilly*, and *Daisy*, and I'm pretty sure there will be more. Perhaps a few might be adopted...*Jeremy, Terah, Jessie*, and *Aaron*. If not mentioned, it's only because, at the time of this writing, you had not entered my world. This book is for you. It's full of my thoughts, dreams, and perhaps a bit of wisdom that I have picked up through the years.

When I was young, I never thought that I would reach the age that I thought was old. Now here I am wondering how life can pass by so quickly. When I look in the mirror, I wonder where the young girl who dreamed of her future went. Why did it not happen the way she had hoped and dreamed? Yet inside that older reflection is a knowing that it all happened for a reason, and despite the twists and turns, the journey is meant to continue, and dreams are still here to dream.

My life has been far from perfect. I've made my share of mistakes. I have lived through pain and rejection, heartbreak and loneliness, sorrow and death. Despite all that, my glass is more than half full, and my Lord has walked with me every step of the way. He and I have overcome each obstacle, and through it all, I have found a joy that only He can give.

In each word that I have written, I pray that you can see this joy and find it in your life as well. You, dear one, are special to me and in my prayers. Open your heart wide as you read. Jesus loves you even more than I do.

Ever since I can remember, I knew of God. I sensed His presence lying in my bed staring out the window as the panes formed a cross. I knew He was with me as I gazed at the stars in my sleeping bag at Camp Pine Springs. I even felt Him when I said my childhood prayers, "Now I lay me down to sleep…"

Just as God always has been and always will be, He makes His presence known every minute of every day. Take a walk outside just to experience His handiwork. Take a breath and know that He is the one that gives you each one. Look up at the starry sky, the vast ocean, the human body, each of them a miracle.

How can we not marvel at a God so mighty? As if creation isn't enough….He gave us free will and a soul and spirit to live forever. Even more, He loves each and every one of us beyond anything we can ask or imagine. Then He sent His son to die for our sins. There is no greater love.

Dear one, feel His love. Breathe in His goodness. No matter what life brings your way, know that God can see you through.

"I will remember the works of the Lord: Surely I will remember thy wonders of old."

Psalm 77:11

This is a book of poems that I wrote during the 2020-2021 pandemic, but they include many thoughts that I've had throughout my life. I dedicate it to my family, my sister's family, my mom and dad, and the many friends whom I have met throughout my life's journey. I wish I could list them all.

Read it all at once, (because I know you won't be able to put it down :)) or use it as a devotional each day. There are over 150 entries in no particular order. It is my prayer that something in this book will resonate in your soul and bless you.

Thank you for taking the time to read it.

TABLE OF CONTENTS

ABIDE

Life hurts at times, people lie
But even then, I will abide.
When someone speaks and makes me cry
I may falter, but I'll still abide.
When sickness takes my friend to die
I'll trust in You and will abide.
Questions linger, and feelings hide
Leaning on You, I will abide.
When the end is not in sight
I'll choose to wait and will abide.
When night overtakes, and I can't see light
I'll rest in your presence and will abide.
No matter the trial, how deep or how wide
I'll trust in you Jesus; I will abide.

You must never count on people to fulfill your needs. Eventually, everyone will let you down. Turn to the One who always listens and loves you unconditionally through every one of life's circumstances. Abide in Him.

"Abide in Me, and I in you. As the branch cannot bear fruit of itself, unless it abides in the vine, neither can you, unless you abide in Me."

(John 15:4)

ADDICTION

Addiction
Am I the only one
Whom temptation taunts this way?
My temporary victories
mock me
As I run back to old ways
And fail
Again, and again and again
The lies overtake my soul
They become who I am
I hate who I've become.
Seeking comfort
I find my drug of choice
But no one knows
It's my little secret
"I'm not hurting anyone but myself."
I say
And I give in again
I hate you Sugar
I'm breaking up with you
Tomorrow.

I used to think that I was the only one in the world who battled with a sugar addiction. As I have become open and vulnerable, I've discovered that I am not alone. The enemy wants us to feel isolated. If we keep our struggles to ourselves, we will remain that way. If we share them with others, we can possibly get the help we need. We may still struggle, but we won't do it alone.

> Praise be to God and Father of our Lord Jesus Christ, the Father of compassion and the God of all comfort, who comforts us in all our troubles, so that we can comfort those in any trouble with the comfort we ourselves have received from God.
>
> **2 Corinthians 1:3-4**

ALL OF ME

You say this body's a temple
I present this temple to You
Clean it up, Lord, take the old
Make it fresh and new.

Take my body, all of it
Laid down in full surrender
Keep my eyes looking straight ahead
My sins to You I render.

Take my mind, my very thoughts
Fragmented within my soul
Piece them back together
To once again be whole.

Take my heart, so broken
Hardened by sin and pain
Dig up all the fallow ground
And make it soft again.

Take my spirit, speak to it
Your words may I embrace
Hold me in Your loving arms
And let me see Your face.

All of me, Lord, take my all
Make me more like You
Wash away the emptiness
Fill me with life anew.

Do you not know that your body is a temple of the Holy Spirit, who is in you, whom you have received from God? You are not your own; you were bought at a price. Therefore, honor God with your body.

1 Corinthians 6:19-20

And So, I Wait

My Lord, my God, You'll always be first
Through the best of times and through the worst
And so, I wait

My heart yearns for love I never knew
A love never-ending that is known by but a few
And so, I wait

Desire awakens within, passion calls my name
I know that if I give in to it nothing will be the same
And so, I wait

Maybe, God will one day allow two hearts to meet as one
Hearts no longer broken, but sought after and won
'Til then I wait

And on that day should it not tarry, I'll present a gift
Of love and peace and purity, it's how I want to live
And so, I wait

The process of waiting can feel like forever, but in light of eternity, it is well worth the wait. So many marriages end in divorce. How can anyone be absolutely sure? Even when you think you're doing everything right, a marriage can fail. Love dies and families are devastated. Wait, my friend, if you're questioning...wait!

> I wait for the Lord, my soul waits, and in his word, I put my hope.
>
> **Psalm 130:5**

FOREVER IN HIS ARMS

I gave him time
Time to heal, time to feel
But he didn't come running back
And so, I'll wait
For a love that doesn't question
Or live in the past
Where love will blossom
Because it's real
Until then
If then ever comes
I'll stay in the arms
Of the one who will never leave
Who will never stop loving me
No matter what
The one who gives me hope
And peace
And joy
There I will stay
Forever in His arms.

All of my life I have desperately yearned to be loved. As a young girl, I thought there was something wrong with me if I didn't have a boyfriend. For a time, I would feel satisfied, but it was never enough. Through the years I have learned that there is only one who can satisfy...my Creator, my Lord, my Savior. He is, and always will be the only one who can fill every need that we all have for love.

> Let the morning bring me word of your unfailing love, for I have put my trust in you. Show me the way I should go, for to you I entrust my life.
>
> **Psalm 143:8**

APPLES OF GOLD

Words aptly spoken, like apples of gold
Are not to be hidden; they're a tale to be told.
These tender words that you could bestow
May bring out feelings, healing tears to flow.
The words may become ornaments of gold
Long unspoken, needing to be told.
Like the coolness of snow when harvest is here
Refreshing a soul to know God is near.
These apples of gold, freely given by some
Will cheer others onward, doubts overcome.
When times are toughest, and it's hard to push through
A word aptly spoken, could make things new.
Speak words of life through apples of gold
Give them freely, and let hope unfold.

Proverbs 18:21 tells us that life and death are in the power of the tongue. My fifth-grade teacher told me, "Susan, you have perseverance." I was ten years old, and I still remember those words. They spoke life to me.

Unfortunately, I still remember some cutting words that were spoken to me or about me as well...we all do. We can speak life into those we meet. How often do we think something kind, but don't say it? We have the power to speak life; let's do it!

> A word aptly spoken is like apples of gold in settings of silver.
>
> **Proverbs 25:11**

AUTHOR OF HOPE

My pages are empty before You now
You write my story, I don't know how
I'm sometimes tempted to look back
Wallow in pity and feel the lack
The "now" is painful, my progress slow
My future is not for me to know
But the author who writes my story, my life
Is not one to leave me in my strife
He knew the ending before it began
He knows the answer that only He can
He's the author of hope, not of fear
And so, I trust Him and hold Him dear
Author of hope, Your words always true
I give the rest of my story to You.

Letting go is one of the most difficult trials in life. We all tend to think that we know what is best. The old saying, "If you want to make God laugh, tell him your plans," has been tested many times in my life. Sometimes I am able to look back and laugh at myself about what I thought was best, and sometimes I'm just plain relieved that God didn't listen to me. The longer that you walk with God the more you will see that He always knows what is best.

I pray that the eyes of your heart may be enlightened in order that you may know the hope to which he has called you, the riches of his glorious inheritance in his holy people.

Ephesians 1:18

AWAKEN

I awaken
Then the birds
Next, the sun
But my soul still sleeps.
Awaken my soul
To see the Son
To feel His embrace
Knowing His presence
Hearing His voice
Awaken, but be still my soul
To listen
To touch His heart
To be
Breathing in His fragrance
His peace
His love
His heart
Awaken my soul
To be
For Him.

I've always been a morning person. I often awake in the middle of the night for no apparent reason. Could it be that God awakens me? Does He want me to pray? Sometimes I do, but sometimes I just want to go back to sleep. At times my soul does the same. I go through my day making quick decisions oblivious to what way God may be directing me to do. Awake my soul, to be, for Him. Help us, Lord, to sense Your spirit, listen, and be obedient to Your calling.

> Awake, my soul! Awake, harp and lyre! I will awaken the dawn.
>
> **Psalm 57:8**

Begin Again

A new day
Yesterday is over
Mistakes made; love lost
Goals unmet, failures counted
But all for a purpose
To learn, to grow, to flourish
Start anew
Give grace to the past
Look ahead
See hope waiting
Feel joy in each moment
Run hard
Run fast
Toward the One who gave His all
Who gives now
Who will always give
When you look, see, and feel
Receive
He's waiting
Begin again.

Whether it's a new year or just a new day, we always have an opportunity to begin again. Don't listen to the old familiar voice that tells you of your failures and inadequacies. Let the past be the past, and as the old saying goes, "Pick yourself up, dust yourself off, and start all over again."

> Therefore, since we are surrounded by such a great cloud of witnesses, let us throw off everything that hinders and the sin that so easily entangles, and let us run with perseverance the race marked out for us.
>
> **Hebrews 12:1**

BELOVED

My beloved
Chosen
An apple of gold
You are so beautiful
My daughter
Washed clean
Your heart, so pure
Hands reaching out
Embracing love
Pouring forth My presence
Walking in faith
My beloved one
I live through you
Joy is yours
You are mine
Beloved

It took nearly a lifetime for me to embrace these words. I could never see myself the way that God sees me. I knew every mistake, every sin, each selfish thought. How could God feel that way about me? But He does. He knows my every thought and deed, yet continues to love me and call me beloved. I will never understand why, but it's all throughout

His word, and I believe it. He feels the same about you, chosen one. Rest in His presence. You are beloved.

> "Let the beloved of the Lord rest secure in him, for he shields him all day long, and the one the Lord loves rests between his shoulders.
>
> **Deuteronomy 33:12**

BESIDES YOU

So much to give
Love overflowing
Stolen, captured, imprisoned
Shattered dreams
A heartbroken to pieces
Yearning for love
Taken so quickly
Only traces remain
With the pain
And memories
Will there ever be
A heart filled with love
That won't abandon me
Besides You?

If you've experienced the pain of a broken relationship, you understand these words. You feel as though you have so much to give, to love, but you've either been misunderstood or rejected. Perhaps it's happened multiple times and you are left questioning, "Why?" Jesus told us that we would have pain in this world, but He also said that he would be with us through the journey. There is nothing that we must go through that He has not already endured.

No one will be able to stand against you all the days of your life. As I was with Moses, so I will be with you; I will never leave you nor forsake you.

Joshua 1:5

BIRTHDAYS

Birthdays
Balloons, parties, fun, and laughter
Presents and games
Celebrating life
The years pass so quickly
We reminisce
The day we once spent with parents
Becomes a day with children
And grandchildren
The fun and games
Turn to honor and blessing
More years behind
Than ahead
But we leave a legacy
Of celebrating life
Then blessing and honor
As we grow closer
To our final celebration.

In our society, we often do not honor the elderly. It's funny how "old" becomes older and older. I used to think 30 was old, then 40, 50, and so on. My 94-year-old mother admits she is old, but she can run circles around some 50-

year-old. In my family, age is honored. Let's be intentional about blessing our older generation. They are worth honoring.

> Remember the days of old; consider the generations long past. Ask your father and he will tell you, your elders and they will explain to you.
>
> **Deuteronomy 32:7**

BITTERNESS

The stab penetrates
The knife twists
Pain is real
Fighting back
She seeks revenge
He needs to feel the pain he caused her
She fights back
Stabbing with her words
As the knife in her heart
Penetrates still deeper
Bitter and angry
Her heart dies
And he moves on.

Revenge never works! Anger and unforgiveness just fester into bitterness. If you've experienced such pain, begin the process of forgiving the person who hurt you. It may take time, and you may feel like the person does not deserve to be forgiven, but do any of us really deserve the forgiveness we've received? If you don't forgive, bitterness will plague your soul. In addition, if you do not forgive, you will not be forgiven by God. Let it go, move on, and live in freedom.

"For if you forgive men when they sin against you, your heavenly Father will also forgive you. But if you do not forgive men their sins, your heavenly Father will not forgive your sins."

Matthew 6:14-15

Blinded

Questions unanswered
Lingering doubts
Defending my hopes and dreams
Letting go
Only to take back
Blinded
Searching for answers
But turning deaf ears
Reaching out for reality
But touching nothing
Blinded
Healing hands
I push away
Taking one more chance
Opening the door, I closed
Feeling my heart shatter
Within
Blinded

I doubt if I'm the only one who has turned a deaf ear to God. Sometimes we know the answer but are unwilling to accept it. At times we may just be too weary with life to search for it or to change. If God is calling you, don't be blinded. He will give you eyes to see and ears to hear if you search for answers with Him.

> Once more Jesus put his hands on the man's eyes. Then his eyes were opened, his sight restored, and he saw everything clearly.
>
> **Mark 8:25**

BROKEN

Broken
Beyond words
Love walked out
With no promise of return
Is hope alive?
I remember long ago
I prayed
But God didn't listen
Or did He?
God, are you there?
I think I need you
I'm sorry
And broken
Will you help me find hope?
And let love return.

Every person on this planet has felt as if God is not listening at some point in his/her life. Enter faith...Trusting in His promises, we must believe that our Father has a purpose for everything that happens. He hears our desperate prayers, but the answers are often different than what we anticipate or for which we hope. Our choice. We can wallow in self-pity or choose to believe that God does answer our prayers.

Let us then with confidence draw near to the throne of grace, that we may receive mercy and find grace to help in time of need.

Hebrews 4:16

Broken to Beloved

Broken
To pieces
By sin of my own doing
Guilt and shame
Betrayal and heartache
Bit by bit put back together
With love and hope
Whole
No longer fragmented
Light shining through the cracks
Blessed
Discovering joy
Radiating its warmth
Giving back what was received
Knowing who I am
And who I will always be
Beloved

God can put all of the broken pieces back together. The beautiful "cracks" that we all have from life can be cracks through which God's light can shine forth. Friend, know that you are beloved right now. Your cracks are part of your journey. Even when we are broken, we can be blessed, and we always have been and always will be beloved.

As He says also in Hosea,

> "I will call those who were not My people, 'My people, and her who was not beloved, 'beloved.'"
>
> **Romans 9:25**

BLESSED

Blessed
I want for nothing
Provisions overflowing
Contentment abounds
Nourishment
More than enough
Shelter
Strong and secure
Peace
Knowing who's in control
Happiness
With plenty of laughter
Love
Knowing no limits
Blessed beyond measure
Forever

Sometimes I just sit in my chair with my cup of coffee and marvel at how good God is to me. He truly has done more than I ever asked or imagined in my life despite my failures and disobedience. I pray, dear reader, that you can take a moment and bask in his unconditional love. His blessings are for you as well.

Now to him who is able to do immeasurably more than all we ask or imagine, according to his power that is at work within us, to him be glory in the church and in Christ Jesus throughout all generations, for ever and ever! Amen

Ephesians 3:20-21

BURIED TREASURE

Soul grasping
For God
But flirting with the world
A heart searching
For His presence
But unwilling
To destroy the idols
Right words spoken
"All is well"
But inside reality calls
Hypocrite!
Walk away from death
From false gods
Search with all your heart
Like the widow who lost the coin
Seek for that buried treasure
And He will be found.

"It's all good," is such a common response in this day and age. What's really going on inside? How often are we honest with our feelings? How often do we go about our day without giving our Creator a second thought? Open our hearts to search for you, Lord, like the widow searched for her lost coin. Oh God, give us the strength to search wholeheartedly. Sometimes it's just easier to give up or carry on in our own strength. Help us to find that buried treasure.

> "Or suppose a woman has ten silver coins and loses one. Does she not light a lamp, sweep the house and search carefully until she finds it? And when she finds it, she calls her friends and neighbors together and says, 'Rejoice with me; I have found my lost coin.' In the same way, I tell you, there is great rejoicing in the presence of the angels of God over one sinner who repents."
>
> **Luke 15: 8-10**

BUT GOD

Each day leaves questions unanswered
What will happen next?
Fear and doubt prevail
In a world of uncertainty
Who can we trust?
But God
Brother against brother
Malice and judgment
Fear and doubt
But God
Lay down all burdens
He understands
Trust over fear
Mercy over judgment
How?
But God

The world we live in often leaves us questioning. The media instills fear, and it is almost impossible to know who we can trust. Discernment is vital. We must discern and make decisions that may or may not agree with others in our world and even others in our family. As hard as it is, we must be careful not to judge others if their viewpoints don't align with ours.

> Do not judge, and you will not be judged. Do not condemn, and you will not be condemned. Forgive, and you will be forgiven.
>
> **Luke 6:37**

CHILDREN

A quiver, a shoot, a heritage
A gift from the Lord
A blessing
Miracle unfolding
Beginning to flourish and grow
Then stumbling and falling
Recovering, thriving
Always learning
Forever teaching
Lessons learned
But failing some
Branching out towards independence
Leaving home behind
Life anew
Children's children
God's miraculous gifts
New beginnings
Never-ending love.

A mother's love can never be underestimated. I remember waiting in anticipation for my firstborn. I loved him before he was even conceived. The moment I laid eyes on him; I was forever changed. I fretted about how I could ever find enough love in my heart to love another as much as I loved him, but my heart grew as each of my children came into this world. The love I felt was overwhelming, and it never wanes.

It is hard to imagine that God can love us even more than we love our children. I believe that I would die for my children. Lord, I pray that they will always know my love for them, but that yours is even greater.

> "Greater love hath no man than this, that a man lay down his life for his friends."
>
> **John 15:13**

FIRSTBORN

So tiny and tender
My first
I remember his faint smile
The softness of his skin
His sweet smell
Holding him for hours
Staring at perfection
Created by God
My miracle
I remember love
So pure and sweet
Complete dependence on me
And I on him
He completed me
Oh, how I yearn
To hold him once more
To kiss away the pain
And see him smile.

I used to want to have thirteen kids (until my second came along). All my life I couldn't wait to become a mom. Some of my most precious moments in my life were holding my infant children and staring at their wonder. I don't know that I've ever felt more love. I wish that I could have made their lives perfect, but that was not the case. They had to learn from their own mistakes and live with some of mine. I thought that perhaps they'd all grow up and live next door, but that's not the case either. I may not be able to hold them in my arms anymore, but my love for each of them will never fade.

No one has ever seen God; but if we love one another, God lives in us, and his love is made complete in us.

FAMILY

Where roots grow deep
To withhold the storms of life
And arms spread wide
To embrace the endless love
Family
Where a hug soothes the heartache
And laughter penetrates the soul
Where words of love
Bring joy to a mother's heart
Family
Where memories are fond
And cherished
Tucked away in each heart
To stay forever
Family
Where love was born
And any place is home
Where you'll never be forgotten
And love will live forever.

I know that there is no perfect family. Some appear that
way but step into their living room or their car on the way to

church sometimes, and you may read a different story. But, as imperfect as we may be, family is forever.

> Give thanks to the Lord, for he is good, for his steadfast love endures forever. Give thanks to the God of gods, for his steadfast love endures forever. Give thanks to the Lord of lords, for his steadfast love endures forever; to him who alone does great wonders, for his steadfast love endures forever; to him who by understanding made the heavens, for his steadfast love endures forever.
>
> **Psalm 136: 1-5**

ROOM FOR LOVE

How could I ever love another
As much as my first?
I remember being fearful
There is no way
But my heart grew
With each babe born
There was more room
For love
As they grew
They found love
My heart grew even more
As each of them
Found their place within
Grafted into the family
And into my heart
Their children
And more to come
Adopted ones too
No need to worry
Hearts grow
There's always plenty of room
For love.

God knew before creation how many would be in each of our families. He knew the amount of love we would need and how big our hearts would have to grow. He also knew the pain and heartbreak some might have to endure. No matter what you've gone through, make room for love and let it win.

And over all these virtues put on love, which binds them all together in perfect unity.

Colossians 3:14

CHOICES

My mistakes...
Can't you learn from them?
But you must make your own.
At first, I'm here
To pick you up
And bandage your knee
But then you're all grown up.
You choose
I let you
And you fall.
It hurts me more than you
I watch from afar and pray
As you try in your strength
To get up
You fall again and again
There's a hand to help you
He'll help you up
And walk with you
Choose Him...
Or fall again.

Adult children still make mistakes. Letting them fall is
one of the most difficult things a parent has to endure. It is a

time of questioning, "How did this happen? They weren't raised this way." But their mistakes don't define them, they shape them. The ultimate choice must be our prayer.

> "Choose for yourselves this day whom you will serve..."
>
> **Joshua 24:15b**

Pray that they choose the one who can pick them up when they fall, and fall they will. Then trust. Trust as He shapes them to become all that He intended them to be.

CHOOSE
(POST ELECTION DAY THOUGHTS)

Country in turmoil
Unrest, division, helplessness
But in His presence
Hope, trust, and peace
Choose...
His sovereign hands
Hold loosely
Pulling us gently
Close to His heart
Lean away
Or rest
Under the shadow
Choose...
He never let's go
He knew the beginning

He knows the end
Worry about the unknown
Or rest in His peace
Choose

Now may the God of hope fill you with all joy and peace in believing, that you may abound in hope by the power of the Holy Spirit.

Romans 15:13

2020

A year that will not be forgotten
Many lived in fear
Everyone endured hardship
It was quite a year.

Yet some were able to see the good
Life slowed down a lot
Instead of what was missing
They saw everything they got.

When loss and pain ran rampant
They put out their faith and prayer
Knowing that their Lord wouldn't give
More than they could bear.

They look back and are grateful
For all that they have learned
Knowing that it was purposeful
Though not for what they yearned.

Life itself is a journey
Hardship will come along
Let's trust in our Creator
He is never wrong.

No temptation has overtaken you except what is common to mankind. And God is faithful; he will not let you be tempted beyond what you can bear. But when you are tempted, he will also provide a way out so that you can endure it.

1 Corinthians 10:13

CHRISTMAS

Childhood memories long gone by
Presents under the tree
Sleep at last, but waking up
With hearts all full of glee.

Passing on these happy times
To children we hold dear
The excitement and the wonder
That we witness every year.

But as we age, the wonder
Ceases just a bit
Expectations enter in
And dreams can go unmet.

We relive the memories
We're saddened that they're past
Where did all the years go?
Why did they go so fast?

Forgive us, Lord, for focus on
The selfish thoughts of "me"
The wonder and the magic
And the gifts under the tree.

Help our minds to focus
On all, that's right and true
Open up our earthly eyes
To see nothing but You.

You in all your wonder
You beneath the tree
You in every gift that's given
You in all we see.

COME HOME

She left
He cries out in desperation
Anger takes over
Hateful words are exchanged
The bottle beckons
It's always helped before
Or has it?
It soothes the pain
Until morning
But nothing has changed
She's still gone
He's still desperate
And the bottle calls again
Will he succumb
Or listen to another call?
A call to come home
To truth and love
Keep calling, Jesus
Come home, son.

I'm not sure that there is anything worse than the pain a mother goes through over a prodigal son or daughter. Our children do not always follow the path we would like them to follow or learn from our mistakes. They each have to live life for themselves, and they make mistakes too. Sometimes their mistakes lead them to deeper heartache. I must remind myself as I write this that Jesus loves them even more than I do. He hears our every prayer, and He too wants them to come back.

"Restrain your voice from weeping and your eyes from tears, for your work will be rewarded," declares the Lord. "They will return from the land of the enemy. So, there is hope for your future," declares the Lord.

Jeremiah 31:16-17

DEMENTIA

I remember
Sitting on the couch, your arm holding me tight
I remember the smell of fresh baked bread
That you tirelessly made
The countless gifts under the Christmas tree
Our talks about love and my future
But you don't
You don't remember that I came to visit
Yesterday
You forgot our talk from an hour past
You don't remember the names of your grandchildren
I miss you
I almost forget how you used to be
Oh, how I wish I could bring you back
To stay
But I can't
It will never be the same
I know it's not your fault
But it's so hard to see you go
So much forgotten
Lost in time
Some day you may not even know my name
But please know

Please remember
You are loved
Forever

People are living longer and longer, so dementia is becoming more and more common. Losing a loved one to dementia is like watching someone die a slow death unable to do anything about it. It's heartbreaking, but God understands. God watched His Son die a long slow death for you and me.

> When Jesus had cried out again in a loud voice, He yielded up His spirit.
>
> **Mark 15:37**

DIG DEEP

Dig deep, Lord
Cultivate my soil
Break up my fallow ground
The dormant fields
Plant your seeds
To grow your plants
To grow your fruit
So, others may know
Let them taste
And see
That You are good
Let my fruit nourish
Give strength
And comfort
Dig deep
So, I will grow.

If God is the farmer, we must allow Him to break up our soil. It is a process, but just as in a garden, the fallow ground must be broken up in our hearts. The old life must be removed so that new seeds can be planted. Allow God to tear out the old and birth the new in your heart. If He breaks up the fallow ground, plants new seed, fertilizes it (you), you will grow and produce the fruit that you were meant to bear.

> When a farmer plows for planting, does he plow continually? Does he keep on breaking up and working the soil?
>
> **Isaiah 28:24**

Drop the Rock

Who will cast the first stone?
Who is without sin?
The grip on the rock loosens
Haughty thoughts
Pride
Judgment
Another stone awaits
Pick it up?
Or look within
Where is humility?
A listening ear?
An understanding heart?
Who will drop the stone
And free the captives
Bound by sin?
Who will become a prisoner
Holding a rock?

When they kept on questioning him, he straightened up and said to them,

> "Let any one of you who is without sin be the first to throw a stone at her."
>
> **John 8:7**

Why are we so judgmental? I know that it saddens the Lord when He sees Christians judging others and casting stones with their words. Are we any different than the Sadducees and Pharisees holding the rock as they judged the adulterous woman? They dropped their rocks. Have we dropped ours? Oh Lord, don't let us be prisoners holding rocks in the judgment of others. Fill us with Your mercy and grace. Help us to speak the truth in love.

Endless Nights

Sleep evades me
I think...
The same thoughts
They spin in my mind
Over and over
I wonder
I question "Why?"
Waiting for an answer
That never comes
I worry
What if?
It's never resolved
I wonder
Sleep still evades me
I think the same thoughts
Over and over and over
I question "Why?"
I worry
I wonder
Then I pray.

I doubt if I am the only one who wakes up in the night thinking the same thoughts over and over. Often I think, wonder, and worry before I even go to the Lord. He has all of the answers, yet often I don't ask for His help. If only I would take my concerns to Him first. The worry would be gone, and I could rest in peace.

> My help comes from the LORD, the Maker of heaven and earth.
>
> **Psalm 121:2**

FEAR

A change is coming and will soon be here
Along with change, sometimes comes fear

Why can't I think as I ought
And take captive every anxious thought?

I trust You, Lord, You know I do
I know that You will see me through

But in the moment, I'm afraid
Of this change of plans, we've made.

Help me, Lord, help me remember
To give You my thoughts in full surrender

And as I give, I now implore You
To keep these thoughts, I lay before You.

Bury them, so they will cease
And fill me with your perfect peace.

Change is inevitable, and with change, anxious thoughts often attack us. Trusting God brings us into His presence. Here, shackles of worry will fall off instantaneously, and we can walk in freedom and trust.

And the peace of God, which transcends all understanding, will guard your hearts and minds in Christ Jesus.

Philippians 4:7

THE RAT RACE

Places to go so quickly
Things to do right now
How will I ever finish?
Can I do it all somehow?

Thoughts that spin are endless
So many decisions to make
I feel like all I do is give
And they just take, take, take.

Deadlines and expectations
It's all so plain to see
I'm doing the very best I can
Please, just let me be.

So, I can take a moment
To breathe His stillness in
To feel His gentle presence
And know His peace again.

Sometimes if you are in the midst of the rat race, you just need to remove yourself for a moment. Perhaps it's at your desk, outside under a tree, or even in the bathroom. Just take a moment and breathe. Look at your moment or problem in light of eternity, and suddenly it will seem quite small. Sometimes we run so fast to achieve when God wants us to slow down and receive.

> I have fought the good fight, I have finished the race, I have kept the faith. Now there is in store for me the crown of righteousness, which the Lord, the righteous Judge, will award to me on that day-and not only to me, but also to all who have longed for his appearing.
>
> **2 Timothy 4:7-8**

FINALITY

Finality
There's something about it
That helps you move on
Even though there's pain
Accepting the truth
Grieving the loss
But searching for hope
Regrets creep in
Shame sometimes follows
But it's over
And forgiveness wins
Hope is just ahead
I'm coming, Hope
Please wait for me
Finality and I have met
We'll be there soon

A chapter in life is over, a new one begins. Don't allow regret or unforgiveness to hold you captive. Both will bind you to the past and blind you to the hope of your future. Allow God to remove the shackles and instill hope that only He provides.

But God will never forget the needy; the hope of the afflicted will never perish.

Psalm 9:8

FINISH THE RACE

Looking behind
The years fled by
Life surreal
How quickly it goes
A new chapter begins
Much sooner than imagined
Rest, peace, adventure, love
A new beginning
Anticipation and hope
It's almost time
The witnesses cheering
I throw off all that hinders
And run with perseverance
His wind at my back
I will press on
Run free
Run hard
And I will
Finish
The
Race!

I was a teacher for many years. I taught in public schools, homeschool, and Christian school. I recently retired and am loving every minute of it.

For me, it's a new adventure, but I want to finish strong. In this race I'm running, I'm getting closer and closer to the finish line. Wherever you are in your race, I encourage you to have perseverance. Train hard, learn your lessons, and finish strong.

> Therefore, since we are surrounded by such a great cloud of witnesses, let us throw off everything that hinders and the sin that so easily entangles, and let us run with perseverance the race marked out for us.
>
> **Hebrews 12:1**

THE GOLDEN YEARS

How long have I been waiting?
Counting the years, months, days?
Cherishing the lasts?
A few tears shed
Leaving family
My second home
Love and support
But many smiles and much anticipation
As I think ahead
The golden years...
Free to do
Free to be
Here, at last, Lord
Just You and me.

Perhaps you have not reached this chapter in your life yet. Let me assure you that there is plenty of life to live after retirement. I may be nearing the end of the book, but I believe that this chapter will be new and exciting. I can't wait for the "happily ever after!"

But those who hope in the LORD will renew their strength. They will soar on wings like eagles; they will run and not grow weary, they will walk and not be faint.

Isaiah 40:31

A Cedar of Lebanon

Make me
A cedar of Lebanon
Strong and true
Producing fruit
In old age
Useful, therapeutic
Medicinal
Woven into strength
Protection from storms
Shade and rest for the weary
Fragrant
Standing tall
Through the storms of life
And when I pass
May I leave behind
A strong tower
A legacy
Of a life well-lived.

I remember fond memories of my grandmother and my dad. Both are gone now, and when they passed, I grieved. But now I can remember them and think of the wonderful memories we made together. They both left a legacy of love.

I felt so special when I was with them, so loved. My desire is to leave a legacy of love to those I leave behind.

> A good man leaves an inheritance to his children's children.
>
> **Proverbs 13:22**

FOR GOD ALONE

For God alone
My soul waits in silence
My rock and my fortress
We shall not be shaken
I shall not be afraid
A prisoner
Of His hope
As I wait
For God alone
My refuge in troubled times
As I trust
I bask in His steadfast love
Filling me
With His presence
As I wait
For God alone.

Psalm 62

FRESH OIL

I stand beneath the tree
The olive tree
Before me is a lamp
To light my way
To lead me on His path
Pour Your oil over me
Anoint me
To anoint others
Fill me to overflowing
To overwhelm others
With Your presence
Use Your healing balm
In me
To heal others
In You
Pour fresh oil into my being
Saturate me
With You

My heart's desire is to take the good news to all I meet. Though I often fail to look for opportunities, sometimes they happen despite me. If we knew the cure for cancer, we'd shout it from the mountaintops. Why are we hesitant to talk about the greatest news anyone could ever receive? Oh, Lord, make us bold. Anoint us with Your presence in this fallen world.

> The Spirit of the Lord God is upon me, because the Lord has anointed me to bring good news to the afflicted; He has sent me to bind up the brokenhearted, to proclaim liberty to captives and freedom to prisoners.
>
> **Isaiah 61:1 (Jesus's words, not mine)**

LIKE A TREE

Like a tree
Planted by streams
Of living water
Grow my roots, Lord
Deep
Make me sturdy
To endure the storms
Spread my branches wide
To be welcoming
May my blossoms bloom
And be fragrant, compelling
Let me bring shade
And comfort
To all who sit at my feet
And may all who rest there
Look up
And see the One
Living in me.

Have we not all sat beneath a tree with long sturdy branches and roots deep within the ground? What comfort. I remember, as a child, playing there and sensing the wonder of God's creation. How I long to give comfort and peace to those the Lord brings into my life like that tree did for me. Our roots must grow deep before we can offer shade and blossoms that will someday produce much fruit.

> "That person is like a tree planted by streams of water, which yields its fruit in season and whose leaf does not wither—whatever they do prospers."
>
> **Psalm 1:3**

Fullness of Joy

Few have found it
But joy is here
You seek
But not for hidden treasure
You ask
But don't wait for it to come
You run the other way
To find it elsewhere
But joy is here
In all its fullness
Smile through the tears
Run away from the past
Embrace hope
Dare to dream
Laugh!!!
Love from your deepest being
Dance on the clouds
Search for that hidden treasure
Know the fullness of joy.

My heart yearns to tell you that joy can be found. Most people understand happiness, but happiness is fleeting. Joy can be forever. It is nothing but pure, unadulterated truth. As we embrace and love the truth that our Lord has revealed, we may rejoice in all that he teaches us and know the fullness of joy.

> He will fill your mouth with laughter and your lips with shouts of joy.
>
> **Job 8:21**

TOWARDS JOY

Healing is near
I smile a gentle smile
One last tear escapes
As I say goodbye to pain and death
I've lived in that land too long
Walk with me, Lord
Keep my gaze forward
Journey with me to the promised land
"What's that?" you say
"Just my bottle of tears."
"Leave it, there's no more need."
I obey
And my smile broadens
Determined
I leave the pain behind
And walk confidently on
In the light of life
Towards joy.

As you may have noticed, I believe that joy is an essential part of a fulfilled life. Joy is what helps me put my feet on the ground each morning and my head on my pillow each night. Joy helps me through the difficult times and overflows through the "happy." Joy reminds me that every day of my life can be fulfilling and that I can radiate my joy to all with whom the Lord sends my way. Choose joy, my friend, choose joy!!!

> "May the God of hope fill you with all joy and peace as you trust in Him, so that you may overflow with hope by the power of the Holy Spirit."
>
> **Romans 15:13**

Joy in Tomorrow

Lord, more than anything
We want Your will
Please speak clearly
So, we know as we're still.

At times it's confusing
And hard to hear You
Emotions take over
And we can't break through.

We ponder, we wrestle
We think we know
But sometimes Your will means
We need to let go.

Sometimes there's heartache
And deep deep sorrow
But we will trust
That joy comes in tomorrow.

Admittedly sometimes it's hard to feel joy in the midst of the hard times. Trust, dear one, that it will come if we surrender all to God. In the Rudolph song, "There's Always Tomorrow" it says that dreams will come true. Life tells us that that is not always the case, but I can say wholeheartedly that joy can come in tomorrow... even today.

> "Those who sow in tears will reap with songs of joy."
>
> **Psalm 126:5**

Choose Joy

There's joy in the laughter
And joy in the pain
Joy in the sunshine
Even in the rain
Find joy in your sorrow
Someday it will cease
There's joy in your struggles
That one day bring peace.
Find joy in your weakness
It'll make you strong
Even in the waiting
That seems so long.
There's joy in disappointment
That causes so much strife
Joy can bring fulfillment
When you keep her in your life
There's joy in loneliness
She'll help it to end
There's no greater blessing
Then joy as your friend.

"The Lord is my strength and my shield; my heart trusts in Him, and I am helped. My heart leaps for joy and I will give thanks to Him in song."

Psalm 28:7

Joy, Please Stay

It's completely over
The door is closed and locked
Why do I still feel drawn back?
As if I'm being mocked?

Memories taunt me
They refuse to fade
I yearn to forget them
But they won't evade.

Joy tries to enter
But I don't let her stay
It's always in my loneliness
That I push her away.

I locked the door behind me
And threw away the key
Joy, please come back
And stay inside of me.

Raw feelings...we all experience them. Sometimes they seem impossible to overcome. It's okay to have a good cry. I've pounded my fists on the ground and sobbed until I didn't think that there was another tear left inside of me to cry. But when it's all said and done, we must accept that life isn't fair and move on. As my beloved mother says, "Put one foot in front of the other. It doesn't do any good to complain." After a good cry, we all need one now and then; begin again, and admit that the glass really is half full.

> Be completely humble and gentle; be patient, bearing with one another in love.
>
> **Ephesians 4:2**

GIVE US THE NOW

Sudden news
No! It can't be!
Shock and denial...
Don't leave us, please
You are so loved
But for you, what is best?
Eternity beckons
God's will prevails
Us...
We pray for a miracle
Complete restoration
Peace
Oh Lord
Don't take him yet
Give us more time
He's yours for eternity
Give us the now.

When my dear brother-in-law had a heart attack quite unexpectedly, these words were penned. He made a miraculous recovery, but it left his family quite shaken. We all knew where he would have gone, but the thought of life without him was almost unbearable. We are not promised another day. Every day is a gift. His experience has caused us all to think about our own mortality and how we should live the rest of our earthly lives.

> And will come forth; those who did the good deeds to a resurrection of life, those who committed the evil deeds to a resurrection of judgment.
>
> **John 5:29**

> All the days ordained for me were written in your book before one of them came to be.
>
> **Psalm 139:16**

THE MIDDLE

The end is near
Or is it?
The middle feels endless
I yearn
I pray
Waiting for the end
That never seems to come
But "Look back ," He says
At other middles
Was there always an end?
Did you grow in those middles?
Did faith arise?
So, press on and trust
There are reasons for the middles
Rest in the middle
Until the end comes.

I'm not very good at waiting. It seems all my life I've had to wait. I waited for Christmas, for love, for something to be over, for something to come. The list could be endless, but in the waiting, there always seems to be a purpose. Oftentimes we don't see the purpose until the waiting is over. So, if you're stuck in the middle and waiting, remember there is a purpose, and the end will come.

> For the revelation awaits an appointed time; it speaks of the end and will not prove false. Though it linger, wait for it; it will certainly come and will not delay.
>
> **Habakkuk 2:3**

GOD'S SPECIAL CHILD

God created each of us
No one is the same
He loves each one dearly
And knows us all by name.

He pondered and picked some chosen ones
And wrote them in His book
But I believe that for a few
He took still another look.

"These are my special ones
I'll only pick a few,"
But he singled each one out
And one of them was you.

An extra dose of kindness
He put into your heart
Patience, joy, humility
Were only just the start.

Next, He added lots of love
Much more than most can feel
And a heart full of compassion
That is so very real.

He said, "This one is faithful
Until the very end
And will be too many
A true forever friend.

When He was finished
I know that He smiled
With each loving thought
Of His special child.

HAPPY

So much sorrow
Years of smiling through the pain
Hoping for a better tomorrow
More pain
But with it, release from bondage
Contentment and peace followed
Even joy
But happy?
Giggly, little girl jumping up and down kind of happy?
I'd forgotten her name
Let alone how she felt
She came by surprise
And made me laugh
She held my hand
She kissed my cheek
We even skipped, twirled, and danced
We became friends
Happy, I'm glad we met
Let's finish this journey together.

> But may the righteous be glad and rejoice before God; may they be happy and joyful.
>
> **Psalm 68:3**

Oh, how I wish that my friend, Happy, could always be around. Life just isn't like that, and that's okay. When the happy times come, we appreciate them all the more. So, when they come, embrace them. Run through a field of wildflowers, dangle your feet in the mountain stream, and eat that piece of chocolate caramel cheesecake with abandon. Allow yourself to make friends with Happy when she comes knocking at your door.

HE KNOWS

Your creator
Dark, light, sun, and stars
The vast oceans
Majestic mountains
Birds in the air
Fish in the sea
He knows
Your every breath
Each thought
The number of your days
He knows
Each hair on your head
Every grain of sand
All of your hopes
Dreams
And fears
He knows.

One can only marvel at the omniscience of God. Our human minds can never grasp it, but how reassuring it is that our Creator does know all and is always in control. The universe is His, and we need not ever worry. He knows.

Even before there is a word on my tongue,
behold, O Lord, You know it all.

Psalm 139:4

HE UNDERSTANDS

Does anyone understand
The loneliness?
The rejection?
Heartache?
"I do," says Jesus
A rock for a pillow
Rejected, mocked, forsaken
Ridiculed
Heartbroken and lonely
Reality slaps me hard
I repent
As self-pity backs off
He bore it all
He understands

So, I face the rejection
And heartache
But I'm not alone
He lives in me
I have hope
He understands.

It's so easy to fall into self-pity. That's where the enemy of our souls wants us to live, centered around ourselves.

When our focus shifts to the Savior and all that He did for us, suddenly our problems seem small. Oh Lord, help us through our difficulties that seem so unsurmountable. Let us redirect our focus on You and put our trust in You.

> There hath no temptation taken you but such as is common to man: but God is faithful, who will not suffer you to be tempted above that ye are able; but will with the temptation also make a way to escape, that ye may be able to bear it.
>
> **1 Corinthians 10:13**

HELPLESS

Far away

Locked out

Pain hiding behind a smile

Wanting help

To take the pain away

But fear invades

The uncertainty, the past

On my knees

I fall into submission

He knows

His arms reach wide

And grace runs deep

My helpless soul

Wants for nothing

As I wait

For whom my help comes from.

> My help comes from the Lord, the Maker of heaven and earth.
>
> **Psalm 121:2**

Haven't we all been in a helpless state? It feels like God isn't listening and prayers will never be answered. But I have learned that when I submit to God, I find His peace. I can rest in the assurance that He loves me and that He hears my prayers. He knows, much better than I, how to help me in my helplessness.

HIS GARDEN

In His garden I find rest
It is here I stay
Trusting that my roots grow deep
And He'll provide the way

The rain is sent when roots are dry
Sunshine fills my soul
He gives needed nourishment
As He makes me whole

Flowers bud and blossom
There's fragrance in the air
As I breathe in life from Him
He takes away each care

Keep me in your garden, Lord
As I seek my way
Fill me completely with your love
It's here I'm going to stay.

If I could be a flower, it would be a sunflower. Not only is it my favorite color, yellow, but it also has deep roots and a strong, sturdy stem. Although it's not known for its fragrance, it stands tall amidst most other flowers in the garden. It turns its face toward the sun (I like to think of the Son). Its beauty is striking and perhaps others are compelled to come to the garden because of it. Lord, make me a sunflower in your garden.

> The Lord will surely comfort Zion and will look with compassion on all her ruins; he will make her deserts like Eden, her wastelands like the garden of the Lord. Joy and gladness will be found in her, thanksgiving and the sound of singing.
>
> **Isaiah 51:3**

HIS GLORY

As the waters cover the sea
His glory covers the earth
From the thought of conception
Long before each birth
His glory spans the horizon
And it will never end
It's in all of creation
And in the heart of friends
His glory is in everything
It exceeds all bounds
Open eyes and behold it
His glory can be found
Listen for the shofar
Glory in every breath
It will last a lifetime
Even after death
Embrace His glory as you live
Feel its warmth each day
Yield to your creator
And in His glory stay.

Glory is defined as magnificence or great beauty. All one
must do is gaze outside at the wonder of this earth to behold

God's glory. Take a moment to see it, breathe it, feel it. His glory is everywhere. Glory to His name.

> On the glorious splendor of Your majesty and on Your wonderful works, I will meditate.
>
> **Psalm 145:5**

HIS PRESENCE

Though I fall
He helps me up
Though I waver
He steadies me
When off the path
He steers me back
Integrity lives in me
I embrace it
And I'm upheld
My God is pleased
As I live in His presence
Forever

Psalm 41:11-12

MY DELIVERER

Troubles surround me
Sins overtake
My heart fails
I am poor and needy
Yet my desire is to do your will
Your word rests in my heart
I talk of your faithfulness
Of all your love
And truth
They protect me
As I seek You
I rejoice and I am glad
I trust in my deliverer
I exalt His holy name.

Psalm 40

MAY GOD ARISE

Like smoke in the wind
Wax before fire
Let the tormentor fall
May God arise!
A father to those with none
A defender of widows
A balm to the lonely
Set the captives free
May God arise!
The procession in view
Singers and musicians
Summon your power, O Lord
Show us your strength
Your power and majesty
May God arise!

Psalm 68

I Trust in You

The Valley of Baca
I pass through
But You are with me
Chilling springs
Autumn rains
Refresh me as I traverse
From strength to strength
My sun and shield make me blameless
A doorkeeper in your house
Better is one day in your courts
Then thousands apart from You
Restore your favor, Lord
I trust in You.

Psalm 84

MY ROCK, MY REFUGE

My heart is faint as I call
To my rock, my tower
He is my refuge forevermore
And I trust Him every hour.

I will always dwell
In the shelter of His wings
I will find my refuge
As my heart forever sings.

Protect my tender soul, Lord
With faithfulness and love
Wrap me in everlasting
Where your presence is enough.

It is there I will always sing
My praises to Your name
And fulfill my every vow
And in Your presence stay.

Psalm 61

FOR GOD ALONE

For God alone
My soul waits in silence
My rock and my fortress
We shall not be shaken
I shall not be afraid
A prisoner
Of His hope
As I wait
For God alone
My refuge in troubled times
As I trust
I bask in His steadfast love
Filling me
With His presence
As I wait
For God alone.

Psalm 62

RESCUE ME

The waters are deep
I am sinking
Into the miry depths
Floodwaters engulf me
As I search for God
Answer me, O Lord
Do not let me sink
Let the goodness of your love
Rescue me
Let your salvation
Protect me
As I praise You in song

As I glorify You
With thanksgiving
Rescue me.

Psalm 69

LIKE LAZARUS

Like Lazarus
Living entombed
Self-pity, heartbreak, death
Dry bones
Waiting
How long?
Is there hope?
He comes
In His time
God will give you
Whatever you ask
If His will
Ask!
Rise again!
Take away the stone
Remove the graveclothes
Let go!

John 11

Some people live life wearing grave clothes. Death seems to follow them throughout their journey. Obviously, I don't mean that literally, but these people see the glass half empty. They feel as though they are not treated fairly and everything just seems to go wrong in their lives. If you are one of those people, remove your graveclothes, let go of your past, and ask God to reveal His will in your life.

HIS TRUTH

The words stab
Tears flow
Misunderstandings
False perceptions
Lies and accusations
The enemy waits
His familiar voice taunts
But no…
Not this time
The truth sets free
I am free indeed
I stand
Knowing who I am
With eyes on Him
My heart grieves
But my soul rejoices
I've been set free
And I will walk and live
In His truth.

I fell prey to the lies of the enemy for much of my life. He always seems to season a little bit of truth and mix it into his lies. He knows our weaknesses and he targets them on a regular basis. I refuse to succumb to them anymore. There is freedom in living in God's truth.

> So, if the son sets you free, you will be free indeed.
>
> **John 8:36**

> Submit yourselves therefore to God. Resist the devil, and he will flee from you.
>
> **James 4:7**

I AM

I AM
Before time
Everlasting
Before creation
Conception
Even thoughts and dreams
I AM
Tomorrow
All plans for our future
Aspirations
End of life
Eternity
I AM

I sometimes wish that I could grasp the enormity of our awesome God. Our human minds can never comprehend Him. But there is also a peace in knowing that He always was, always is, and always will be. He loves each of us infinitely more than we can imagine, and He has everything under His control. We can rest in the assurance that He holds us in His everlasting arms. He is the great I AM!!!

The eternal God is your refuge, and underneath are the everlasting arms.

Deuteronomy 33:27

I Am Who I Am
Says I Am

I am
Who I AM?
Says I am
And I am chosen
I am a daughter of the king
I am beloved
I am whole
I am beautiful
I am anointed
I am forgiven
I am blessed
I am fearfully and wonderfully made
I am the apple of His eye
I am precious in His sight
I am His
I am
Who I AM
Says I am.

Most of my life, I battled negative thoughts about myself. I'm not pretty enough, I'm so stupid, I'm fat, the list goes on. I read in the word what God said about me, but I just couldn't own those thoughts. It was easy for me to believe them about other people but not myself. I'm still a work in progress, but I'm starting to believe. It's so freeing! Believe these truths; God thinks these things about you too.

> Let the beloved of the Lord rest secure in him, for he shields him all day long, and the one the Lord loves rests between his shoulders.
>
> **Deuteronomy 33:12**

GOD OF THE BREAKTHROUGH

When the enemy shouts
"There's no hope; you don't matter"
I will throw down those lies
And they will shatter.

When he taunts me with words
Of fear and shame
I will trust in God's promises
Through all of the pain.

When hope seems lost
Of dreams once shared
I dispel the lies
That God doesn't care.

And when he whispers
In that voice I despise
I stand on the truth
No more listening to lies.

God of the breakthrough

Heal my heart

Do it completely

Not just in part.

Then you will know the truth, and the truth will set you free.

John 8:32

I Choose Joy

You offer hope, he only shame
You say to trust, he plays a game
He offers nothing, You call me by name
Will it change or remain the same?

The lies are whispered, the choice is mine
Will I accept them and be blind?
Live in pity, continue to whine
Put on a mask and say, "I'm fine."

Or will joy come to stay?
Will it remain, not just for today?
Will it embrace me or stay at bay?
I say to joy, "Please find a way."

Yes, joy is offered, the choice is mine
I won't be bitter or resign
I'll trust in His promises, no longer blind
I choose joy, and now I'm fine.

You turned my wailing into dancing; you removed my sackcloth and clothed me with joy, that my heart may sing to you and not be silent. O Lord my God, I will give you thanks forever.

Psalm 30:11-12

I Just Want a Friend

Surrounded by smiling faces
Laughter echoing in my ears
I am in their midst
And I'm fighting back tears.

I'm alone in the crowd
Why can't they see?
Please someone notice
Won't you see me?

Please look beyond
All the ones in your space
To see if there's someone
Who needs an embrace.

Please look inside me
Is this how it will end?
Give me a chance
I just want a friend.

I've always had a lot of friends. I cherish every one of them. I remember once when a new lady entered my world. I felt as though I just didn't have time for another relationship, but I reached out to her anyway. Little did I know that she would become one of my closest friends whom God has used to speak into my own life many times. Look beyond the outward appearances or the busyness of life. There's always room for another friend.

> Dear friends, since God so loved us, we also ought to love one another.
>
> **1 John 4:11**

I Need You

I need you in the hard times
When my mind is filled with fear
To sense your loving presence
And know that you are near.

I need you in the questioning
When I am filled with doubt
And my mind is ever wondering
What this life is all about.

I need you when I'm angry
With thoughts, I shouldn't say
And when somebody hurts me
And I want to run away.

I need you in the painful
When all I do is cry
And trusting seems impossible
As I just question, "Why?"

But just as much I need you
As every day I strive
To rest in your contentment
And keep my joy alive.

I need you, Lord, I need you
Each moment, draw me near
As I trust your holy presence
And know that You are here.

But I am poor and needy; yet the Lord thinketh
upon me: Thou art my help and my deliverer;
make no tarrying, O my God.

Psalm 40:17

IF I SHOULD DIE

If I should die
Before I waken
Trust that the Lord
My soul has taken
Don't grieve for long
Every tear'll be gone
I'll live with the Lord
And be singing His song
The love we shared
Won't be forgotten
We'll know it again
When we're with His begotten
We'll meet again
It won't be that long
We'll all be together
And singing His song.

I know where I am spending eternity; do you? Dear One, we are all given a choice in our earthly lives. We can either accept or reject Jesus Christ as Lord and Savior of our lives. If we accept Him, we can be assured that we will spend eternity with Him. If there's any doubt in your mind, admit that you are a sinner, ask God to forgive you of your sins, and accept

Him as your Lord and Savior. It's the most important decision that you will ever make. You can use these words to guide you. "Father, I know that I am a sinner. Please forgive me of my sins. Thank you for sending your Son, Jesus, to die on the cross so that my sins can be forgiven. I ask you to come into my heart and be Lord of my life so that I can spend eternity with you."

If you prayed this prayer, please tell someone. Find a good church where you can be encouraged by other believers. Your life will never be the same.

> For God so loved the world that he gave his one and only son that whoever believes in him shall not perish but have eternal life.
>
> **John 3:16**

IMMANUEL

Immanuel, God with us; we can't ask for more
Our Creator, Savior, Comforter, all that we adore.

He's with us in the sunshine and with us through the rains
The long and lonely winter and when it finally wanes.

He's with us on the mountaintops and the valleys oh so deep
The rocky hills before us seem forever steep.

He's with us when we fall in love and when love breaks our
heart
He's with us through the sickness when death calls some to
part.

He's with us through the lonely though we often do not see
He's with us through our apathy and when we bow a knee.

Help us know your presence, Immanuel, our King
Wipe away the stains of life, and help our souls to sing.

Immanuel, God with us; we can't ask for more
Our Creator, Savior, Comforter, all that we adore.

The virgin will be with child and will give birth to a son, and they will call him Immanuel which means, "God with us."

Matthew 1:21

In Between

The valley
So painful, full of grief
I cannot stay
I see the mountaintop
Far in the distance
Will I ever reach it?
It seems I can't go on
I want to sing again
To shout and dance
But I'm in between
Where God seems silent
And all I do is wait
"Rest," He whispers
Find my peace
And joy
When it's time
We will walk out of "In Between"
And find the mountaintop
Together
We'll sing and shout
And dance.

If we could only live on the mountaintops. Then we could look behind into our past and ahead into our future. If we really had a chance to see what lies ahead, would we really want to know? We might see exciting times full of successes and adventures, but we would also see the pain of heartbreak and death. Maybe it's okay to live in the "In Between" trusting God throughout our journey.

> Wait for the LORD and keep his way, and he will exalt you to inherit the land.
>
> **Psalm 37:4**

DANCE WITH ME

The beat is slow and somber
More than one tear escapes my eyes
Disappointment envelops me
The question, "Why?" consumes my mind
Despair beckons me
Wallowing in what could have been
Sorrow lingers and begs to stay
In a moment, God speaks
Will I listen?
The heartbreak is real, but He offers a breakthrough
"Crush disappointment," He says
"Trust in My promises
Shake off despair
Embrace My hope
Listen to the music
And dance with me."

Sometimes life just isn't fair. I'll bet you've heard that a time or two. Disappointment is just something we will have to face whether we like it or not. God never said that our lives would be easy, but He promises to walk with us along the way. If we truly trust in Him, we can find joy in the midst of disappointment. That's not to say that we will not cry ourselves to sleep on more than one occasion. Our emotions are real, but joy can be found. Look for it, it might even take you a day or two to find it, but it's there.

> "Weeping may last through the night, but joy comes with the morning."
>
> **Psalm 30:5**

INTENDED TO BE

If I could change my past
And all God meant for me
I wouldn't be who I am
And whom I was intended to be.
Maybe there wouldn't be shame
And certainly, no guilt
But there would be no repentance
Upon which my foundation was built.
There'd be no need for confession
I might have a lot of pride
I doubt if I would realize
The price Jesus paid when He died.
If I hadn't had the hard times
Or handled them all on my own
I wouldn't see my need for Him,
I'd do it all alone
If I'd never been rejected
And felt the pain of death
I might take life for granted
Until my final breath.

Thank You, Lord, for everything
Now I can clearly see
That life has grown and shaped me
Into whom I was intended to be.

All of life has a purpose. The sooner we accept this and allow God to work His purposes in our lives, the better off we will be. I believe that everything that happens in life is for a purpose. Embrace each heartache, every joy, each rejection, each success...all for a purpose. All for His glory!

> But the plans of the Lord stand firm forever, the purposes of his heart through all generations.
>
> **Psalm 33:11**

INTO THE DEEP

A spring
Bubbling up
A new life beginning
Pouring forth into more
Strength and surety
Into the deep
Another spring
After the winter thaw
And another
After the summer storm
Each new beginning
Each source
From deep within
Carried away
With purpose and determination
Into the deep
Where waters calm
And rest is found.

Life's trials give each of us an opportunity. When God is living inside of us, we can find Him. Only He can give us the rest we so desperately need. Search for Him, dear one, and live in the calm waters that only He provides.

"And you, my son Solomon, acknowledge the God of your father, and serve him with wholehearted devotion and with a willing mind, for the LORD searches every heart and understands every desire and every thought. If you seek him, he will be found by you; but if you forsake him, he will reject you forever."

1 Chronicles 28:9

KNOWING GOD

I remember lying in bed and seeing
The cross that formed
In the window panes of my childhood home
I laid in silence
Knowing God
Nestled in my sleeping bag
Under the starry skies
Silently
Knowing God
Rising forth out of the river
Sins forgiven
Life beginning anew
Knowing God
Weeping over a heartbreak
Death and betrayal
Abandonment
Knowing God
Alone in the morning
Bible in hand
Peace and contentment
Knowing God.

We are only fooling ourselves if we say that there is no God. He makes himself known to all of us. He never said that life would be easy, and sometimes it's just not, but, my friend, He is as real as the air we breathe. Take the time to look for Him and He will be found.

> But if from there you seek the Lord your God, you will find him if you seek him with all your heart and with all your soul.
>
> **Deuteronomy 4:29**

LAST LOVE

Safe and secure
Loved
The past has passed
The now...wonderful
Learning, playing, dreaming
The future...coming soon
With surety and love
Doubts have vanished
Questions are answered
Dreams on the horizon
Within reach
Joy inside
Radiating happiness
Love is real
My last love...
So glad I waited
And opened my heart.

With many years behind me, I've had lots of opportunities for love. In my life, though I wanted it to be different, it never lasted. The pain of heartbreak followed, and after numerous failures, it was frightening to think about trying again to open my heart. But I did. Love is a choice every day. It's never 50/50, but 100% at all times. The choice to love is ours.

> "A new command I give you: Love one another. As I have loved you, so you must love one another. By this everyone will know that you are my disciples, if you love one another."
>
> **John 13:34-35**

LIKE THE WIDOW

Give
Out of abundance
The firstfruits only?
Or like the widow
Who gave it all
From the heart
To the poor and needy
With reckless abandon
Have I given enough
To feel the lack?
And trust
That needs will be supplied?
Or do I hold too tightly
To security
Let go my hand
Be free my heart
To give
Like the widow.

In America, in the age of prosperity, it's hard to let go. We have so much, yet we hold on to what we have as though we have nothing. If you've ever had the joy of seeing someone blessed by your generosity, or if you've ever been the recipient of someone else's gift, you'll understand the joy that can be found in giving. Lord, let go our hands and free our hearts to give.

> Each of you should give what you have decided in your heart to give, not reluctantly or under compulsion, for God loves a cheerful giver.
>
> **2 Corinthians 9:7**

LONELY

Just lonely
And me
Seems he's around a lot
Always by my side
Wanting to hang on
He's a heavy burden
I can't seem to shake
A cold wet blanket
A dark threatening cloud
Of gloom
He has almost become
A part of me
But for God...
In my despair
He is there
His presence comes
He knows my pain
And cries with me
He wraps me in His comfort
Goodbye Lonely
I don't want you anymore.

I'm a people person, so loneliness often tries to haunt me. Sometimes, even when people surround you, you can feel lonely. When I'm lonely, I talk to Jesus. I think of Him on the cross, beaten and mocked, forsaken temporarily by His own Father. Yes, I think His loneliness was far worse than mine. We are never alone, and He will never leave us or forsake us.

> "The Lord himself goes before you and will be with you; he will never leave you nor forsake you. Do not be afraid; do not be discouraged."
>
> **Deuteronomy 31:8**

LOST LOVE

Fighting back tears
Wondering why
Dreams shattered
Was it all a lie?

Memories fresh
Of how love was taken
Will I trust again
Or be forsaken?

Heal my heart, Lord
Make it new
Your will be done
I trust in You.

I've had my share of love in my life, or at least what I thought was love. What young girl doesn't dream of her first love lasting forever? It rarely does, and if you escape the pain of a broken heart, consider yourself blessed. But life marches on, and healing comes at last. God can restore those broken hearts and make them new again.

When I am afraid, I put my trust in you. In God, whose word I praise, in God I trust; I shall not be afraid. What can flesh do to me?

Psalm 56:3-4

HEARTBREAK

Throughout the day
I walk in peace
But when I sit
Alone with my thoughts
I feel the pain
When will it go away?
Why did this happen?
The tears have ceased
But my heart still grieves
The dreams have faded
But questions remain
And with them... pain
Thoughts of all that could have been.
I'm not sure
If my heart can break
Any more.

Few escape the pain of lost love. It is a part of life. Some, like myself, have experienced it more than once. I love easily and fully, so heartbreak can be devastating. Sometimes, rather than dealing with the pain, we build walls. Walls prevent us from loving fully and experiencing the joy of true love. Life is too short to live halfway. Ask God to heal your broken heart, forgive, and love with abandon!

> Love is patient, love is kind. It does not envy, it does not boast, it is not proud. It is not rude, it is not self-seeking, it is not easily angered, it keeps no record of wrongs. Love does not delight in evil but rejoices with the truth. It always protects, always trusts, always hopes, always perseveres.
>
> **1 Corinthians 13:4-7**

A Love
That Will Endure

As I lay my head down
And tears run down my face
I think of all the shattered dreams
As I long for your embrace.

I knew I had to let you go
It just feels so surreal
But when I was away from you
I knew it wasn't real.

And so, I said goodbye
To the one, I held so dear
I said farewell to hope
And now I'm left with fear.

Fear of letting go again
Fear of love too deep
Fear of being blinded
When my mind goes to sleep.

Lord, set a guard around my heart
As I begin anew
Let me learn to trust
And find a love that's true.

And so, in full surrender
Here's all that is unsure
I know it will be worth the pain
For a love that will endure.

LOVE

Like dawn
Spreading over the mountain
Love grows
Slowly bringing its light
To an open heart
An ember
Softly burning
Creating warmth
That brings peace
Spreading from within
A knowing
Enveloped in arms
That won't let go
Safe and sure
Sensing the heartbeat
Of the other
Where you're home
And you never want to leave.

Love is a choice, and it doesn't always look like what we think it should. Give it time. A beautiful friendship can grow into lasting love. Sometimes love hides and takes us unexpectedly. Look past the outward appearance and you will see deep into the soul. It's so worth searching for. It will feel like home, and you will never want to leave.

> The Lord does not look at the things man looks at. Man looks at the outward appearance, but the Lord looks at the heart.
>
> **1 Samuel 16: 7b**

WONDERING

If he
If I
Will he?
Will I?
Can he?
Can I?
When?
Where?
How?
Should he?
Should I?
Does he?
Do I?
Maybe
Maybe not
I wonder

One thing that I hope I've learned through my many mistakes is to wait until the wondering is over. Sure, we all wonder what our future will be like, but wondering "if" is a sure sign to wait. When doubts enter into a relationship, wait. Either they will go away or they will remain. If they remain, stop wondering and move on. Don't ever wonder, "What if?"

My son, if you accept my words and store up my commands within you, turning your ear to wisdom and applying your heart to understanding, and if you call out for insight and cry aloud for understanding, and if you look for it as for silver and search for it as for hidden treasure, then you will understand the fear of the Lord and find the knowledge of God.

Proverbs 2:1-5

GOODBYE

I can't take away your pain
Though it would be for your gain
I cannot give joy to you
You must seek and receive it too.
I gave you my all, you know I tried
It wasn't enough, and a part of me died
But I'll go on; content I'll be
With no more insecurity
I'll find a love that looks ahead
Where love is present and the past is dead
I pray that you too find this peace
Where love will bloom and sad will cease
I will try to stop asking why
But it is time to say goodbye.

Saying goodbye to someone you care about can be devastating. Whether it is a break in a relationship, a move, or death, it's a loss. It's especially hard when saying goodbye hurts someone else. But, on the other hand, sometimes it's just time to put things on hold or end them altogether. Saying goodbye often means, like the apostle Paul, that we may not ever see that person again. Perhaps, as one chapter ends, a new one is about to begin.

They all wept as they embraced him and kissed him. What grieved them most was his statement that they would never see his face again. Then they accompanied him to the ship.

Acts 20:37-38

TRUST AND SEE

Thank you, friend
For your kindness
Your affirmation
Some good laughs
Feeling comfortable
I like you a lot
And you like me
I trust you
And you trust me
We both trust God
And now we'll wait
And like
And trust
And see.

Aww, yes, the beginning of the next chapter. It's all exciting and new, but it's a little scary as well. There are many wounds that may still be healing. If you've been wounded, trust will undoubtedly be an issue. Some say that time heals all wounds. I'm not sure that I agree...some linger in the deep and only reveal themselves when conflict arises. I do know that trust takes time, so time is our friend in any relationship.

A little patience sprinkled into the time would benefit any new beginning.

> Surely you desire truth in the inner parts; you teach me wisdom in the inmost place.
>
> **Psalm 51:6**

LOVE AGAIN

How many times
Can a heart be broken
And pieced back together?
Afraid of loving again
Rejection, abandonment, sorrow
Yet yearning for love
Fear of the heartbreak
Or breaking someone else
A wall could be built
To protect
Hard, impenetrable
But walls can't feel
Lord, guard my heart
Without walls
Help me to listen
To Your holy whispers
Make me quick to hear
Slow to speak
And feel
But let me feel
Open my heart
To love again.

How can a young man keep his way pure? By guarding it according to your word. With my whole heart I seek you; let me not wander from your commandments! I have stored up your word in my heart, that I might not sin against you.

Psalm 119:9-11

LOVE CAME

Years of longing
Hope deferred
Committed to waiting
Alone
Rejection and heartache
Pain almost unbearable
But with it, full surrender
And fruitful growth
Contentment was born
And peace
But deep within, the longing moaned
Then he came
At first, I didn't see him
I was blinded
But his warmth enveloped me
And soon I knew
I'd found my home
Now love remains
And is here to stay.

It is a rare gift to find a love that lasts. If you know that love, I hope that you know what a beautiful treasure you have. If you are still waiting for it, it's worth the wait. Always remember that each moment, every breath, each word spoken, or act of service done is a choice. Regardless of whether the other person chooses to love or not, the choice is yours. God chooses to love us unconditionally. There is no love that can even compare to His love for us.

> And may you have the power to understand, as all God's people should, how wide, how long, how high, and how deep His love is. May you experience the love of Christ, though it is too great to understand fully. Then you will be made complete with all the fullness of life and power that comes from God.
>
> **(Ephesians 3:18-19)**

Waiting for Love

Walls crumbled
A few scattered pieces left behind
To build a solid foundation
Arms open wide
To receive
Any blessings
Sent my way
Heart softened
Tender
Broken in places
But pieced back together
To be whole
Mind guarded
To look for signs
Or warnings
Spirit willing
Waiting
Waiting
Waiting
For love

Let the morning bring me word of your unfailing love, for I have put my trust in you. Show me the way I should go, for to you I lift up my soul.

Psalm 143:8

LOVE FOUND ME

I closed the door
And walked away
Temptation taunted me
I looked back
But not for long
Fate came
Slow and steady, sure
Like an ember softly glowing
Emulating warmth
And peace
Then I saw love
Up ahead
I hardly recognized him
Could it be
That he found me?
And took me by surprise
Here I am, Love
I'll hold your hand.

Love is patient, love is kind. It does not envy, it does not boast, it is not proud. It does not dishonor others, it is not self-seeking, it is not easily angered, it keeps no record of wrongs.

1 Corinthians 13:4-5

Love, Joy, Peace, and Jesus

Love
In your arms, I'll stay
Speaking words that heal
Sending pain away

Joy
Fill me to the brim
Flowing ever out of me
Living life for Him

Peace
Bring me to your peace
His gentle presence
Where all worries cease

Jesus
I know You'll never leave
I will walk beside You
As to your heart, I cleave.

MASKS

The words I speak, I try to feel
But deep inside, my pain is real
I put on my mask over my frown
I tell myself that I'll come around
I see the smiles, I feel an embrace
But the smile isn't real upon my face
Help me, Lord, heal my heart
Heal me fully, not in part
Help me trust You in full surrender
Remember, Lord, my heart's still tender
Show me patience as I heal
Those words I speak, help me to feel
Remove my mask, help me to smile
Do it soon, Lord, it's been a while.

If you've lived through a pandemic, you are quite familiar with masks. Oftentimes though, we put masks on when they are not a requirement. We don't want anyone to know that we are not perfect. We fear rejection or judgment. If we could all take off our masks and be vulnerable, we would find out that there are others out there who may be experiencing the same thoughts that we have. How freeing it is when humility takes over and we share our imperfections. Perhaps then there would be a smile under your mask.

But he gives more grace. Therefore it says,

> "God opposes the proud, but gives grace to the humble."
>
> **James 4:6**

MEETING KINDNESS

I met a man the other day
Some might say he's old
But he embraces kindness
With his heart of gold.

His body is giving out on him
He brings his walker along
But kindness leads him on each day
He doesn't stop singing his song.

His wife of many years by his side
Proves that it is true
You're not too old to hold love dear
And share some kindness too.

He's humble but has purpose
He lives to the fullest each day
And when age pushes back at him
He looks for another way.

Thank you, Kindness, for not growing old
For telling the world to give
Fully, completely, don't give up
Love 'til the end and live

Therefore, as God's chosen people, holy and dearly loved, clothe yourselves with compassion, kindness, humility, gentleness and patience.

Colossians 3:12

Melt My Heart

Stabbing words
Blaring horns
Quiet whispers and stares
Undeserved gestures
Misunderstood judgment
Motives unclear
Why Lord?
Difficult people
So hard to love
But You did
"Look beyond," you say
Hurting people
Hurt people
Love your enemies
Love even ones who hurt
Love beyond measure
Melt my heart, Lord
To be like yours.

Some people are hard to forgive let alone love. But God tells us to love, so we need to love. We certainly don't always know the path these people have had to walk. Life can wear blisters on people's feet, and that can be painful. Try to see past the pain and love them just for who they are. That's the love of God.

> But I say to you, love your enemies and pray for those who persecute you.
>
> **Matthew 5:44**

MERCY

Your mercy is good
It overwhelms my being
I don't deserve it

But you pour it forth
Undeserving as I am
Filling me with praise

All you bore for me
That I didn't have to bear
Because of mercy

I love You, my Lord
My lips will sing your praise
Your mercy is good.

Mercy is defined as compassion or forgiveness shown towards someone whom it is within one's power to punish or harm. Mankind, in this fallen world, deserves nothing because of our sin. Yet God, in His infinite mercy, sent His Son to die on the cross so that our sins could be forgiven. Let us never take for granted His mercy.

Because of the Lord's great love we are not consumed, for his compassions never fail. They are new every morning, great is your faithfulness.

Lamentations 3:22-23

MY ALL IN ALL

Creator
All knowing
All powerful
Always everywhere
Eternal
My Alpha and Omega
Within
And all around
Before
And behind
My Comforter
My Peace
My All in All

Sometimes I need to redirect my thoughts to how small I am and who God really is. In reality, I am less than a speck of sand or a blink of an eye. When I begin to wonder why the world is not revolving around me, I try to see myself compared to the universe or eternity. Yet God in His infinite glory created each of us for a divine purpose, and He loves us infinitely. He knows our thoughts before they even enter our minds. He knows our fears, our doubts, and every sin, yet He loves us still. Even when we sin, again and again, He knows and loves us. If you ever doubt His love, meditate on the fact that God sacrificed His one and only Son for a broken and fallen world.... for you and for me.

> But God demonstrates his own love for us in this: While we were still sinners, Christ died for us.
>
> **Romans 5:8**

MY DAUGHTER

Long before you were conceived
God knew I needed you
I'll never forget the day we met
When I saw that it was true
A girl, a beautiful girl
Of my very own
Such happiness and wonder
Unlike I'd ever known
Holding you in my arms
As tears ran down my face
Gently stroking every part
As I cherished each embrace
I watched you grow and wondered
How God could love me so
That He could give me such a gift
Of my very own
My little babe, all grown now
God's loving gift to me
I'll always hold you in my heart
Throughout eternity.

We had decided that our quiver was full. Four boys seemed like enough, but God knew better. One of the happiest days of my life was the day that my Annie was born. She was and still is my dream come true. I cannot express in words the love between a mother and a daughter. I thank God for her every day.

> I have not stopped giving thanks for you, remembering you in my prayers. I keep asking that the God of our Lord Jesus Christ, the glorious Father, may give you the Spirit of wisdom and revelation, so that you may know him better.
>
> **Ephesians 1:16-17**

MY FOREVER FRIEND

All that I have You've given me
The good and the bad, so I could be free
Trusting in You that it's all for my good
And loving me fully as only You could
You've walked beside me for many years
Through joy and laughter, heartache and tears
You've always provided more than I need
And as I followed, You would lead
When I fell, You lent a hand
And gave me strength so I could stand
I trusted, yet I faltered too
But You were there to see me through
Ever faithful to the end
Lord, You're my forever friend

I treasure my friendships. God knew that I needed friends, so He gave me a lot of them. But no person could ever compare to the friendship of our heavenly Father. Time with Him refreshes the soul. He, and only He, can fill you with streams of living water. Blessings will flow as we give Him the gift of our time. Peace will be the anchor of your soul.

A sweet friendship refreshes the soul.

Proverbs 27:9

Surely you have granted him eternal blessings and made him glad with the joy of your presence.

Psalm 21:6

MY FRUIT

Love, wrap me in your arms
Joy, dance with me
Peace, flood my being
Patience, hold my hand
Kindness, guard my tongue
Goodness, pour yourself into my soul
Faithfulness, walk beside me every step
Gentleness, kiss my cheek
Self-control, please linger
My fruit
May others be drawn
To its beauty
May it be sweet to the taste
Satisfying
To the soul
An aroma
Of my Creator
A refreshing breath
Of His being
A beautiful medley
Of my God

But the fruit of the Spirit is love, joy, peace, forbearance, kindness, goodness, faithfulness, gentleness and self-control. Against such things there is no law.

Galatians 5:22-23

MY HIDING PLACE

Behind the closed door, alone with Him
Reading His word, filled to the brim

Listening intently to His voice
Hearing Him speak as I rejoice

Grateful always for this life I'm living
Thankful for each breath I'm given

Waiting for the answered prayer
Though I don't know when or where

Fighting battles on my knees
Trusting in His victories

This is where I rest my soul
Where I see He will unfold

Here I'm filled with love and grace
Living in my hiding place.

I have a special chair where I always sit to be alone with God. It's by a window where I can look outside and see flowers blooming in the summer and a grassy field blowing in the wind. It makes me feel connected to God. That's my hiding place. I hope, dear reader, that you have a hiding place as well.

> But when you pray, go into your room, close the door and pray to your Father who is unseen. Then your Father who sees what is done in secret, will reward you.
>
> **Matthew 6:6**

My Mansion

Each broken piece
Brought tears and pain
But I knew that there
I could not remain.

I will forgive
And He'll restore
The trust, the love
And so much more.

Broken pieces
Now made whole
Allowing the healing
To reach my soul

As we build back
Stone by stone
I watch the structure
Become my own.

For me...a mansion
Strong and tall
With no more need
Of a protective wall.

I see it now
As plain as day
Where hope abides
And I will stay.

A WALL TO A
MANSION

Looking about me
I see pieces of my wall
Scattered all around
Here I am in the midst of them
I was broken, I am healing, and I will overcome
Each piece has purpose and hope
A foundation has already been laid
A firm foundation
One that cannot be shaken
And with His help we rebuild
He and I
Each broken piece we bind together
One on top of the other
I see progress, hope
Instead of a wall
We build a mansion
I shall reside there
With purpose, dreams, and hope.

We are all in the process of building or rebuilding. Metaphorically speaking, sometimes God needs to remove a few of the stones that we put into our wall. If we allow Him to, He takes those stones and rebuilds them into a beautiful mansion. Someday we will live there for eternity. Oh God, break down our walls and build our heavenly homes.

Do not let your hearts be troubled. Trust in God, trust also in me. In my Father's house are many rooms; if it were not so, I would have told you. I am going to prepare a place for you. And if I go and prepare a place for you, I will come back and take you to be with me that you also may be where I am. You know the way to the place where I am going.

John 14:1-4

MY REFUGE

Under His wings
In His presence
My refuge
His span covers all my stains
His warmth encompasses me
Soft and gentle
Protecting
Nurturing
Providing
I rest
Trusting in His provisions
Hidden under His grace
Knowing His love
As I take shelter
Under His wings
All my days.

There are few things more beautiful to me than holding a sleeping baby in my arms. The babe, so peaceful, understands my comforting touch. He trusts completely and receives the love provided. Our Heavenly Father offers this refuge to us. He loves us far more than we can love the babe in our arms, and He is a far greater provider. Oh Lord, let us rest in your presence, under Your wings, all of our days.

> He will cover you with his feathers and under his wings you will find refuge; his faithfulness will be your shield and rampart.
>
> **Psalm 91:4**

MY WALL

I didn't want to feel the pain
So, I built a wall
I didn't cry anymore
I couldn't or I'd fall
I couldn't love fully
I just didn't feel
My heart was numb
My pain was real
But You removed my stony heart
You knew it couldn't stay
You broke it into pieces
And took it all away
Now I feel the sorrow
But I also feel deep love
Tearing down the wall
Was a gift from God above.

When we are hurt, we tend to build protective walls. We don't want to ever hurt this way again, so we erect a wall to keep us from future pain. From my experience, this doesn't work. The pain needs to be felt, wounds need to be healed, people need to be forgiven. If we don't knock the walls down, we will walk around in a state of numbness and we will also not be able to feel all of the love and joy that is offered to us.

> No longer will violence be heard in your land,
> nor ruin and destruction within your borders,
> but you will call your walls Salvation and your
> gates Praise.
>
> **Isaiah 60:18**

I am Free

Imprisoned within the walls
I built
Myself
Each stone carefully hewn
Rejection, self-pity, pain
God, help me!
Is that a fissure?
A crack where light shines through?
Hope enters
I look up
And with the touch of His feather
The walls crumble
Hope envelops me
And with it enters trust
I raise my hands toward heaven
"Live, laugh, love," He says
I am free!

NOW

Past is over
"Don't look back ," some say
But what if we do?
Face the regret and shame
Look heartbreak in the eye
Dispel fear
And run
Courageously
Forward
The past becomes
A source of hope for the future
Where lies the land of the living
Unending joy
And even if it's not felt now
Your "now" can become your future hope
Run
Courageously
Forward
Embrace the now
Your source of hope.

How often do we look back at our past and think, "If only..." Where do those thoughts take you? Do you live in regret? Does discouragement take hold and make you wonder if there's any hope? Don't allow the enemy of your soul to steal your joy. Oh, Lord, give us the strength to learn from our mistakes. Give us the courage to face our future without fear. Help us to accept You as our source of hope. Fill us with Your joy.

> For I know the plans I have for you, declares the Lord, plans to prosper you and not to harm you, plans to give you hope and a future.
>
> **Jeremiah 29:11**

NOW AND THEN

Sometimes now is hard
I want then
When now is over

At other times now is wonderful
I want to stay
And not let it end

I must live in the now
Trust in the then
Be present where I am
As I walk from now to then

Then will come
When now is over
So, I wait...
Until then.

Patience is not my strongest suit. Waiting is often difficult and at times my impulsiveness can take over. We all want to be happy, but in reality, we often have to wait for it, and sometimes it just doesn't come. We must learn to be content in our "now." "Then" will eventually come, and with it contentment, and perhaps happiness as well.

I have learned to be content whatever the circumstances. I know what it is to be in need, and I know what it is to have plenty. I have learned the secret of being content in every situation whether well fed or hungry, whether living in plenty or in want.

1 Corinthians 4:12

OLD FRIENDS

Our path together
May not be long
But we're walking
Toward the Son
We may encounter a weed or two
And just maybe
An adventure awaits
But there will always be time
To sit on a bench
With the Son in the background
And just be
With each other.

Very few things give me more joy than time with a friend. Now that I have entered my "golden years," I realize that time may be short. I've already lost some precious ones that I won't see again on this side of heaven. As the old song goes, "Make new friends and keep the old. One is silver and the other's gold." How precious is the gift of friendship...just being with each other.

Greater love has no one than this, that one lay down his life for his friends.

John 15:13

PROSTRATE

Prostrate I lie
Before You now
Prostrate I fall
Laying down my burdens
But also, my dreams
They are yours
All of them
I surrender
For you know best
I lay at your feet
In humble submission
Reverential fear
Unable
To reach out and take back
All laid down
Prostrate I lie
Before You now
Prostrate I remain.

There came a point in my life when I realized that God knows better than me. I fought it for a long time, planning my life and thinking that my plan was best. Laying everything before God and allowing Him to be in control is really quite a relief. His ways are far better than ours.

> "For I know the plans I have for you," declares the LORD, "plans to prosper you and not to harm you, plans to give you hope and a future. New Living Translation. For I know the plans I have for you," says the LORD. "They are plans for good and not for disaster, to give you a future and a hope.
>
> **Jeremiah 29:11**

> Ezra blessed the LORD, the great God, and with uplifted hands, all the people responded, "Amen! Amen!" They bowed down and worshipped the LORD prostrate on the ground.
>
> **Nehemiah 8:6**

My heart is faint as I call
To my rock, my tower
He is my refuge forevermore
And I trust Him every hour.

I will always dwell
In the shelter of His wings
I will find my refuge
As my heart forever sings.

Protect my tender soul, Lord
With faithfulness and love
Wrap me in everlasting
Where your presence is enough.

There I will always sing
My praises to Your name
And fulfill my every vow
And in Your presence stay.

Psalm 61

REJECTION HOLES

Rejection leaves a hole
Each one leaves more space
For God, an opportunity
To fill each one with grace
Holes no longer empty
But lovingly restored
Gently filling each of them
No need to be implored.
Filled to overflowing
Now with grace to give
No longer rejected
But with purpose to live.
Life unto the fullest
Rejection holes now filled
Looking back, able to see
His good and perfect will.
Pain and rejection
Helped make me who I am
Now grace and compassion
All part of His plan.

I believe that rejection is one of the most painful things
we encounter in life. It's a betrayal beyond measure...usually

by someone whom we care for deeply. It involves acceptance and ultimately forgiveness. Many people struggle with acceptance. Forgiveness is even more difficult because oftentimes the one who rejected us does not seek forgiveness. We are left with a decision of whether we will forgive the other person or not.

The person who rejected us is not affected by whether or not we forgive him/her. But we are. Harboring unforgiveness will lead to bitterness. Even a small amount of bitterness will affect your outlook on life. Rejection can mold you into someone who is compassionate, empathetic, and understanding. Don't allow rejection to make you bitter; allow it to make you better.

> We've been surrounded and battered by troubles, but we're not demoralized; we're not sure what to do, but we know that God knows what to do; we've been spiritually terrorized, but God hasn't left our side; we've been thrown down, but we haven't broken.
>
> **2 Corinthians 4:8-9 MSG**

Rescue Me

The waters are deep
I am sinking
Into the miry depths
Floodwaters engulf me
As I search for God
Answer me, O Lord
Do not let me sink
Let the goodness of Your love
Rescue me
Let Your salvation
Protect me
As I praise You in song
As I glorify You
With thanksgiving
Rescue me.

Psalm 69 (paraphrased)

Most of us have moments that we remember of absolute desperation. I remember pounding my fists on my bed crying out, "Where are you God? Why? Why? Why?" I didn't know if I could breathe another breath, and I sobbed until I thought that I didn't have any more tears left within me. Feelings need to be expressed, and crying out to God is the best way to express them. He can take our raw emotions and begin the process of healing and restoration. Cry out to God, my friend. In Him there is hope.

SET APART

Set aside?
Rejected?
Or...
Set apart
And called
To fulfill a destiny
Each his own
Listen
When He calls
Go forth
He is in
And works through you
You...
Not set aside
But set apart
For His purposes
Your destiny

We all have a past. We've all been through rejection and heartache, and it never gets any easier. Know that God understands, and has a reason for everything that happens. We don't know what awaits tomorrow, but we know that He will walk through it all with us. He is ever present and ever mindful of our destiny.

> So, I reflected on all this and concluded that the righteous and the wise and what they do are in God's hands, but no one knows whether love or hate awaits them.
>
> **Ecclesiastes 9:1**

SISTER LOVE

Longer than anyone
You've known my entirety
And loved me
We exchanged clothes
And secrets
And fingers over "the line"
We whispered and giggled
And argued and fought
And loved
Remember being Miss America?
Our late night talks and dreams?
Our weddings
Our children
The laughter
The heartbreaks and tears
Walking and talking
And listening too
So many memories
Love like no other
Thank you, my sister
My forever friend.

If you are blessed enough to have a sister, you'll understand these words. Sisters just "get" each other. No one can erase the memories, and no one can replace a sister's love. My sister, Linda, is a double sister. We are sisters by birth and sisters in the Lord. She will always be a double blessing to me.

> Whoever claims to love God yet hates a brother or sister is a liar. For whoever does not love their brother and sister, whom they have seen, cannot love God, whom they have not seen. **21** And he has given us this command: Anyone who loves God must also love their brother and sister.
>
> **1 John 4:20-21**

SNOWFLAKE

Did you know
That not one snowflake is like another?
Each one created unique
And when examined closely
So beautiful
Some perfectly formed
Some slightly imperfect
All beautiful
Just like us
Why can't we see ourselves
Like snowflakes?
Pure and lovely
Bringing beauty to a fallen world
Though imperfect...
Perfectly imperfect
As the Creator intended
Fall, beautiful snowflake
Land with purpose
Spread your beauty
To your world.

For you created my inmost being; you knit me together in my mother's womb. I praise you because I am fearfully and wonderfully made; your works are wonderful; I know that full well. My frame was not hidden from you when I was made in the secret place. When I was woven together in the depths of the earth, your eyes saw my unformed body.

Psalm 139: 13-15

Song of Love

I remember as a little girl
Sensing your love for me
Melting my childlike heart
So, I'd be forever free

That's when I fell, fell in love, fell in love.
I fell in love with you.

I recall coming out of the water
My sins washed whiter than snow
A new life within me beginning
A love that continued to grow.

Deeper I fell, fell in love, fell in love.
I fell in love with you.

All through life we've journeyed
You always by my side
Every day I love you more
With you, I'll forever abide.

'Cause I fell in love, fell in love, fell in love.
I fell in love with you.

Beloved, let us love one another, for love is from God, and whoever loves has been born of God and knows God.

1 John 4:7

Speak to Me

Speak to me, Lord
So, I can hear
Louder than a whisper
And I'll hold Your words dear.

Give me discernment
To listen with my mind
To hope in the future
And leave the past behind.

Help me to learn
From all the times I've lost
Give me the strength to try again
And I won't count the cost.

Push me, Lord, to persevere
When life just feels too bleak
Open up my heart and soul
And let me hear You speak.

God speaks to His children. My friend, if you cannot hear His voice, ask Him to open up your heart to receive Him. Repent of your sins, ask Him to cleanse you, and pray that He will become your Lord and Savior. Your life will never be the same. It is the most important decision you will ever make. Let's spend eternity together!!!

> My sheep hear My voice, and I know them, and they follow Me.
>
> **John 10:27**

BE STILL MY SOUL

Be still my soul and feel His peace
Bask in it; let worries cease
Know that God is in control
Life doesn't have to take its toll.

Be still my soul, so I can hear
His gentle voice to silence fear
His spirit as it envelops me
Taking over my humanity.

Be still my soul, and feel His love
Surrounding me from up above
Guide me to the ones in need
So always to His voice, I heed.

Be still my soul that I may know
Your love and peace so it will flow
Out of me that I can bless
Others with my happiness.

I am often reminded as I walk through my house to be still. The words "Be still and know" are on the walls of my bedroom and living room. Could it be that I need reminders to allow God to be God and not take matters into my own hands? To be honest, when I try to make things happen the way that I want them to, my track record has not been great. Do you think that maybe the God of the universe might know what's best for you and me? Help us to be still, Lord, as we wait for You.

> "Cease striving and know that I am God; I will be exalted among the nations, I will be exalted in the earth."
>
> **Psalm 46:10**

Steadfast and True

Sure, as I am that You are real
I know that I will always feel
Strength radiating from my soul
To carry me forward and make me whole.

My Lord, my God, steadfast and true
I will forever walk with You.

I know that all your words I will heed
No matter where my path may lead
From early morning into the night
From lowest low to the highest height.

My Lord, my God, steadfast and true
I will forever walk with You.

Perhaps I'll stumble; at times I'll fall
But I will answer when You call
I'll get up and start anew
I can do all things with You.

My Lord, my God, steadfast and true
I will forever walk with You.

I can do all things through Christ who strengthens me.

Philippians 4:13

THANKFUL

For the joy
It radiates my soul
For the blessings
I count them every day
For provisions
They give me surety
For love
It fills my heart
For peace
It walks with me
For trials
They make me strong
For heartache
It fills me with compassion
For unanswered questions
They test my faith
For Jesus
For everything
Thankful

If you've never read the book, <u>One Thousand Gifts</u>, by Anne Voskamp, I would highly recommend doing so. She challenges the reader to be grateful in all circumstances and to begin a journal of 1,000 things for which you are grateful. At the current time, I am on number 3,651 and believe me, there are many more to come. Looking at your circumstances through a thankful lens will change your life.

> This is the day that the Lord has made, let us rejoice and be glad in it.
>
> **Psalm 118:24**

BLESSED

Blessed
I want for nothing
Provisions overflowing
Contentment abounds
Nourishment
More than enough
Shelter
Strong and lush
Peace
Knowing who's in control
Happiness
With plenty of laughter
Love
Knowing no limits
Blessed
Beyond measure
Forever.

We often take for granted how blessed we are. We live in a country where we receive ten times the income of an average person in the rest of the world. We have freedom of speech, press, and religion. We own our own homes and know where our next meal will come from, yet often we grumble and complain. Sometimes we just need to take a step back and count our blessings.

> Every good and perfect gift is from above, coming down from the Father of the heavenly lights, who does not change like shifting shadows.
>
> **James 1:17**

THANKS

For the flowers, birds, and trees
The moon, the stars, the sun
For fellowship and laughter
And all the family fun.

I'm thankful, oh so thankful
For all that I hold dear
For friendships and neighbors
That I see throughout the year.

I'm thankful for the memories
Of those who have passed on
The smiles of special times gone by
Even though they're gone.

If I counted all my blessings
It would take more than a day
So, I'll keep them in my heart
And forever they will stay.

And giving joyful thanks to the Father, who has qualified you to share in the inheritance of his holy people in the kingdom of light.

Colossians 1:12

THRIVE

When life is difficult
Do wedding bells ring?
Can we see light?
Are we able to sing?
Questions unanswered
Unprecedented times
Are there crops in the fields
And grapes on the vines?
Fear conquers many
They've lost their way
Will we move on
Or with those thoughts stay?
In these hard times
Of push and pull
Is the glass half empty
Or is it half full?
Will we give in to
Just being alive
Or will we trust God
And learn how to thrive?

Though the fig tree does not bud and there are no grapes on the vines, though the olive crop fails and the fields produce no food, though there are no sheep in the pen and no cattle in the stalls, yet I will rejoice in the Lord, I will be joyful in God my Savior.

Habakkuk 3:17-18

THE ALABASTER JAR

Did you wonder if you should?
The cost was great
What will they say?
What will they think?
Or did love compel you?
Great love
Like none you'd ever known
Did you look into His eyes?
Surely there were tears
What did you feel
As you gave your greatest gift?
Your all
For your All in All
Does His fragrance still linger?
Can you still see His eyes of gratitude?
I know you'd do it again
And so, would I.

> While he was in Bethany, reclining at the table in the home of Simon the Leper, a woman came with an alabaster of very expensive perfume, made of pure nard. She broke the jar and poured the perfume on his head.
>
> **Mark 14:3**

It's easy to say that I would do the same, and at the moment, maybe I would. But every day, do I give my all to the One who gave His all for me? Is He always before me in the forefront of my mind, or do I leave Him "at home" forgotten as I run around performing all of my important duties? Do others smell His fragrance because I've given my all to Him and His aroma lingers? What about you? Would you break your alabaster jar for Him?

THE DIAMOND

Intense heat
Extreme pressure
Years and years and years
A crystal of hope forms
Is there beauty beginning to shine?
More heat and pressure
Life is hard
But deep within
Strength grows
Searching for it
It seems endless
Discovering
A beauty so rare
That when revealed
It is magical
Reflecting the light
Of its Maker

Do you know anyone who has been through the most difficult of times, yet walks uprightly with strength and dignity? They are the diamonds of this world. Their brilliance shines and their beauty is unmatched, but their strength and beauty did not come easily. These diamonds are rare. If you know one, consider yourself blessed. If you are one, thank you for shining so brightly and reflecting God's light.

> Dear brothers and sisters, when troubles of any kind come your way, consider it an opportunity for great joy. For you know that when your faith is tested, your endurance has a chance to grow. So let it grow, for when your endurance is fully developed, you will be perfect and complete, needing nothing.
>
> **James 1:2-4**

THE FOOT
OF THE CROSS

Standing tall, I could do it all
Walking with pride right by my side
I always embraced the breakneck pace
Never run down nor wearing a frown
Couldn't be beat as I resisted defeat
Much to achieve if you believe
You make the rules, don't be such fools
Life is great, and that's your fate

Then one day I found my way
I saw the lie and had to die
To all the pride I held inside
I was the fool with my made-up rules
For God to use, I had to lose
When I finally fell, then all was well
My soul laid down, new life I found

I wandered in the wilderness; I once was oh so lost
Then I laid my soul at the foot of the cross

No more wandering; I'm no longer lost
My soul will stay at the foot of the cross.

If Jesus is our friend, we should be willing to lay down our lives for Him. He died for us. We should be willing to live for Him.

"This is my commandment, that you love one another as I have loved you. Greater love has no one than this, that someone lay down his life for his friends. You are my friends if you do what I command you."

John 15:12-14

THE PRODIGAL

He walked away
Long ago
Deceived by the world
And hypocrites
We all failed him
Except You
But he blames You
He hasn't come back
Yet
Oh, Prodigal
Come home!
I'm watching for you
Come feast with me
You are welcome
Forever loved by me
And the one who would leave the ninety-nine
For you
Come home
Do you hear us calling?
Come home!

Does everyone know a prodigal? How my heart breaks
each time I pray. How many years have I spent on my knees

now? Sometimes I feel so helpless, but I know God wants the prodigals, and His love is even greater than a mother's. I know that God hears my prayers, so I continue to cry out to Him. Lord, soften the hearts of the prodigals, let them find humility, and bring them home.

Call to the east and the west, claim this promise, that God will gather those who have scattered! Pray that God leads them when they have purposefully shut their eyes so they cannot see his path.

> "Since you are precious and honored in my sight, and because I love you, I will give men in exchange for you, and people in exchange for your life. Do not be afraid, for I am with you; I will bring your children from the east and gather you from the west. I will say to the north, 'Give them up!' and to the south, 'Do not hold them back.' Bring my sons from afar and my daughters from the ends of the earth-everyone who is called by my name, whom I created for my glory, whom I formed and made." Lead out those who have eyes but are blind, who have ears but are deaf.
>
> **Isaiah 43:4-8**

Coming Home

Your arms outstretched
Beckoning, "Come!"
I retreat...it's been a while
Are You really there?
You persist, "Come!"
Once again, I question
But You don't leave me there.
Ever
"Come!"
This time I run
Your arms envelop me
I bury my head in Your chest
Tears succumb
You weep with me, for me
Because You understand
Then You wipe away my tears
I'm coming home!

A Mother's Prayer

"Return to me,"
Says God
Remember the days of youth
When He called your name?
You tried to hear
But the cry of your pain
Was louder
Abandoned, forsaken, left behind
Hypocrites everywhere
Imperfect people
Always
He still calls
Years of your mother's painful prayers
Feel empty
Forgive
Return
He's still calling
Please listen.

> Therefore I tell you, whatever you ask in prayer, believe that you have received it, and it will be yours.
>
> **Mark 11:24**

THE PROMISED LAND

Your promises
You tell me in your word
That they are coming
As all my life I've heard

Your return
You spoke and I believe
Though at times I falter
To those words, I'll cleave

Your strength
To get me through each day
To walk ever beside me
And help me not to stray

Your love
You'll hold me in your arms
Pouring You into me
Keeping me from harm

Your faithfulness
You'll always hold my hand
Until I take my final steps
Into your promised land.

In My Father's house are many dwelling places; if it were not so, I would have told you; for I go to prepare a place for you. If I go and prepare a place for you, I will come again and receive you to Myself, that where I am, there you may be also.

John 14:2-3

THE SEASONS OF LIFE

Summer is over
Peaceful days, starry nights
Sunbeams and rainbows
Autumn arrives
Vibrantly colored leaves
Gentle breezes
Warm blankets and campfires
Then the long winter
Cold and lonely evenings
Dreary days
Storms on the horizon
Will it ever end?
But spring breaks through
Promises of life again
Cleansing rain
Life anew
Give us this reminder, Lord
Through the seasons of life
If summer can't endure
Help us through the cold and lonely storms of winter
Though we're dormant, grow our roots

Give us strength to look ahead
To see life, start to bloom
With hope for another summer.

"While the earth remains, seedtime and harvest, and cold and heat, and summer and winter, and day and night shall not cease."

Genesis 8:22

THE VEIL

The veil torn
No more separation
Need I ask why I am torn too?
Each muscle
Every sinew
That keeps me separated
Torn
My heart ripped to pieces
Each tear brings pain
And as I'm torn
I bleed
Just like Him
But then I heal
I'm made new
No longer separated
No more veil.

Once there was a veil that separated us from God. When Jesus died, the veil was torn. Jesus died for our sins... my sin, your sin. Why should we not be torn a bit too? He wants to tear our sin right out of our hearts. It hurts, but in the end, there is no more separation...no more veil. Oh, Lord, show us where we need to be torn. Forgive us our sin as we forgive others. The veil has been torn.

Therefore, brothers, since we have confidence to enter the Most Holy Place by the blood of Jesus by a new and living way opened for us through the curtain, that is, his body, and since we have a great priest over the house of God, let us draw near to God with a sincere heart in full assurance of faith, having our hearts sprinkled to cleanse us from a guilty conscience and having our bodies washed with pure water.

Hebrews 10:19-22

TIME

Time
Always ticking
How much is left?
When will it end?
Never our own
To control
Waiting
For it to pass
Hoping
For it to come
Wanting more
Or maybe less
Time
Will there be enough?
Or too much?
Always with us
Or maybe not.

The older I get, the harder it is for me to fathom time. As a child, it seemed that I was always looking forward to Christmas or my next birthday. Now I am constantly thinking, "Where did all of the time go?" We are not promised another day, and I want to make the most of the days I have left. Lord, may this be our prayer. Father, may my time be yours. Please give me the time I need to do Your will in my life.

> There is a time for everything, and a season for every activity under heaven: a time to be born and a time to die, a time to plant and a time to uproot, a time to kill and a time to heal, a time to tear down and a time to build, a time to weep and a time to laugh, a time to mourn and a time to dance, a time to scatter stones and a time to gather them, a time to embrace and a time to refrain, a time to search and a time to give up, a time to keep and a time to throw away, a time to tear and a time to mend, a time to be silent and a time to speak, a time to love and a time to hate, a time for war and a time for peace.
>
> **Ecclesiastes 3:1-8**

TRANSFORMED

On a mountain
Transformed
Enveloped in a cloud
Purity
This is my Son
Whom I love
Listen to Him
Let your heart
Be transformed
Enveloped in love
Purity
Peace
This is my Son
Whom I love
Listen to Him.

God tells us in His word that when we are saved, we are a new creation; old things pass away, and all things become new. He transforms us by the renewing of our minds. As we become new, we can embrace His purity and peace. We do this by listening to His still small voice and becoming obedient to His calling.

Therefore if any man be in Christ, he is a new creature: old things are passed away; behold, all things are become new.

2 Corinthians 5:17

TRUTH

Failure calls my name
You did it again
Will you ever learn?
You'll never change
Might as well give up
The all too familiar voice
Beckons me once more
All lies!
Another voice whispers
Still and small
Grace
Receive it
Mercy
New every morning
Love
Unconditional and never-ending
Truth
I'm listening to you.

I listened to lies most of my life. There's the truth behind the lies, and our enemy is quite convincing. But God, in His infinite mercy, can dispel all lies. Stand firm in the truth that He speaks. It will set you free!

> "Then you will know the truth, and the truth will set you free."
>
> **John 8:3**

Unfailing Love

People
So, flawed
Dysfunctions, disorders, labels
Excuses, fear
Liars
Deceivers
Unable to trust
Or fully love
But the cross...
Burdens laid down
At His feet
Fears dispelled
Excuses bound
Truth no longer withheld
Trust reborn
Unfailing love
Jesus

We all have issues, and most of us have lots of them. Everyone wants to figure out the answers. We search, but often in the wrong places. There is only one answer to all of the questions, and that is faith in Jesus Christ. He doesn't always tell us the answers, but He directs us towards them if we submit to Him. Jesus is our answer.

> So that the proof of your faith, being more precious than gold which is perishable, even though tested by fire, may be found to result in praise and glory and honor at the revelation of Jesus Christ.
>
> **1 Peter 1:7**

UNWAVERING

So easily pulled away
Compromise, distractions, apathy
Usual vices
Escape
Ignoring reality
Am I a great pretender?
I need you, Lord
Give me strength
Courage to fight
Passion to live fully
Clothe me in dignity
Dressed in Your righteousness
Step by step with You
My shepherd
Lead me on
Unwavering

Sometimes I wonder if I will ever arrive. I used to think that I was a pretty good person, but as I grow older in the Lord, I see more and more of my inadequacies. I smile my best smile, but inside I know that I'm often distracted, apathetic, and I tend to compromise. It's a good thing that I have a Father in heaven who loves me unconditionally and who will always be with me to spur me on. You too, my friend, fight the good fight.

> "Fight the good fight of the faith. Take hold of the eternal life to which you were called and about which you made the good confession in the presence of many witnesses."
>
> **1 Timothy 6:12**

VOWS

Vows
Do we mean what we say?
Promises of forever love
Dabbing at a tear
A smile that won't fade
Until...
Doubts appear
Unkind words are spoken
Love fades
Was it really there?
You need more
You deserve better
And you listen to the lies
Leaving behind
Promises of forever
That fade into yesterday
Gone forever
Without a care.

About half of the marriages today end in divorce. I grieve every time I hear that a couple is going through one, and I know God does as well. Yet, I do not stand in judgment. I have sincerely meant the vows that I have spoken in my life, but they have not all been fulfilled. Sometimes we make mistakes, at times there are reasons to break a vow, and always we can be forgiven. But broken vows always bring pain, so consider carefully before you make one.

> If a man vows a vow to the Lord, or swears an oath to bind himself by a pledge, he shall not break his word. He shall do according to all that proceeds out of his mouth.
>
> **Numbers 30:2**

WORDS

First words
Hello
It's nice to meet you
Friendships made
Some pass quickly
Others form deep bonds
Words of affirmation
Validation
Words of love
Sometimes regret
Never able to take back
Words can part souls
It's over
Goodbye
Or restore
I miss you
Come back
I'm sorry
Forgive me
Your final words
Will they part souls
Or restore?

We should all think carefully before we speak. How many times has something come out of our mouths that we wish we could take back, but the damage is already done. Thank the Lord for grace. We cannot take our words back, but we can ask for forgiveness allowing relationships to be restored. If there is a breach in any relationship, the words "I'm sorry" go a long way.

> And the God of all grace, who called you to his eternal glory in Christ, after you have suffered a little while, will himself restore you and make you strong, firm and steadfast.
>
> **1 Peter 5:10**

You Are Not Alone
(for the Single Mom)

Alone
With kids
After heartache and rejection
Feeling worthless, used
Afraid
What will happen?
Who can I trust?
When will this be over?
Where will I go?
Why me?

He is with you
He is all you need
You can trust Him
He will provide and guide
He will always love you
He will never leave
Your maker is your husband
You are not alone.

If you find yourself as a single mom, your journey will no doubt be challenging. You will ask many questions and wonder why. There may be times of self-pity, but this time can also be a time that you draw close to God. The most difficult times in my life are when I saw the most growth. It's those times of desperation when I truly learned to trust God. He never failed.

> For your Maker is your husband— the LORD Almighty is his name— the Holy One of Israel is your Redeemer; he is called the God of all the earth. The LORD will call you back as if you were a wife deserted and distressed in spirit— a wife who married young, only to be rejected," says your God.
>
> **Isaiah 54:5-6**

Young at Heart

As a child
Old was young
I passed that young old
Long ago
Many years behind me now
Old is so much older
I'm still young
At heart
Old is nursing homes
And dementia
Maybe someday I'll be old
But now
I'm still young
At heart
Will I use a walker?
Will I forget my children's names?
Maybe I'll be old then
But I'll still be
Young at heart.

Life is surreal sometimes. I remember my great Aunt Katherine saying, "The days go slowly, but the years fly by.

The older I get, the more I realize the reality in that statement. Time goes quickly. Cherish it while you can.

> "To everything there is a season, and a time to every purpose under the heaven: a time to be born, and a time to die; a time to plant, and a time to pluck up that which is planted; a time to kill, and a time to heal; a time to break down, and a time to build up; a time to weep, and a time to laugh; a time to mourn, and a time to dance; a time to cast away stones together; a time to embrace, and a time to refrain from embracing; a time to get, and a time to lose; a time to keep, and a time to cast away; a time to rend, and a time to sew; a time to keep silence, and a time to speak; a time to love, and a time to hate; a time of war, and a time of peace."
>
> **Ecclesiastes 3: 1-9**

FINAL THOUGHTS

Every feeling felt
Each word penned
Somehow it feels complete
Perhaps more to come
But for now, I rest
My gift I give
To those I love
Words at times unspoken
But heartfelt within
To you, the special one
I give these words
My heart
My soul
My love
You are so dear to me.

Made in the USA
Middletown, DE
09 January 2022